P9-DHT-738

3 9082 06

Withdrawn

Northville District Library
212 W. Cady Street
Northville, MI 48167-1560

Withdrawn

INTRODUCTION TO GERMAN POETRY

INTRODUCTION TO GERMAN POETRY
A Dual-Language Book

EDITED BY

Gustave Mathieu & Guy Stern

DOVER PUBLICATIONS, INC.
New York

Copyright © 1959, 1987 by Dover Publications, Inc.
All rights reserved under Pan American and International Copyright Conventions.

Published in Canada by General Publishing Company, Ltd., 30 Lesmill Road, Don Mills, Toronto, Ontario.
Published in the United Kingdom by Constable and Company, Ltd., 3 The Lanchesters, 162–164 Fulham Palace Road, London W6 9ER.

This Dover edition, first published in 1991, is an unabridged and updated republication of the work originally published under the title *Invitation to German Poetry* by Dover Publications, Inc., New York, 1959.
This edition is also published together with a cassette entitled *Listen & Enjoy German Poetry* (ISBN: 0-486-99929-7).

The following poems and translations in this collection are reprinted by the kind permission of their publishers and authors:
"Der Arbeitsmann" by Richard Dehmel from *Gesammelte Werke*. Through the kind permission of Vera Tügel-Dehmel.
"Du schlank und rein wie eine flamme" by Stefan George from *Gesamtausgabe der Werke*. Verlag Helmut Küpper, Düsseldorf, Germany.
"Der Vater" by Albrecht Haushofer from *Moabiter Sonette*. Lothar Blanvalet Verlag, Berlin, Germany.
"Ich liebe Frauen" by Hermann Hesse from *Die Gedichte von Hermann Hesse*. Suhrkamp Verlag, Frankfurt am Main, Germany.
"Die Beiden" by Hugo von Hofmannsthal from *Gesammelte Werke*. S. Fischer Verlag, Frankfurt am Main, Germany.
"Die Entwicklung der Menschheit" by Erich Kästner. Atrium Verlag, A.G., London, England.
"An den Leser" by Franz Werfel from *Gesammelte Gedichte*. S. Fischer Verlag, Frankfurt am Main, Germany.

Manufactured in the United States of America
Dover Publications, Inc., 31 East 2nd Street, Mineola, N.Y. 11501

Library of Congress Cataloging-in-Publication Data

Invitation to German poetry.
    Introduction to German poetry / edited by Gustave Mathieu & Guy Stern. — Dover ed.
        p.   cm. — (A Dual-language book)
    Previously published as: Invitation to German poetry.
    ISBN 0-486-26713-X
    1. German poetry—Translations into English. 2. English poetry—Translations from German. 3. German poetry—History and criticism. 4. Poets, German—Biography. 5. German poetry. I. Mathieu, Gustave, 1921– . II. Stern, Guy, 1922– . III. Title. IV. Series.
PT1160.E5I68 1991
831.008—dc20   90-23242
                                                                          CIP

Northville District Libra.
212 W. Cady Stree   NOV 0 3 2001
Northville, MI 48167-156

3 9082 08356 7753

Contents

Introduction

German lyric poetry, more than any other literary form in which the German mind and genius have expressed themselves, has entered the main stream of the world's cultural heritage. This is primarily due to the fortunate circumstance that the German lyric reached its greatest flowering at approximately the same time as did German music. The rare result of this felicitous marriage between word and tone was the *Lieder* of such nineteenth-century composers as Beethoven, Brahms, Schubert, Schumann, Wolf, Mahler, and Mendelssohn. But German poetry also found world-wide recognition through numerous student songs, many of which were written by well-known poets. The international language of music succeeded in conveying and sometimes even enhancing aesthetic values which were apt to be lost in mere translation. Thus many German poems overcame all linguistic barriers in the form of songs.

But innumerable German poems which have not travelled abroad on the wings of song — and these exceed by far those which have — may be appreciated on their own merit as independent works of art. Ever since Goethe and the Romantics, German poets have striven to make music with thoughts and words; the greatest succeeded in evoking by these words an almost magical *Stimmung* or mood. Contrary to the often-held belief, the German language is not harsh, clumsy, or heavy. In lyric poetry, it has proved itself as pliable a medium as any other language. Many of the selections in this anthology demonstrate the astonishing smoothness, elegance, and melody of the German language, and reveal in a small way the German poets' great concern with the musical effects of alliteration and assonance, of rhyme and rhythm.

In form too, German poets cultivated a wide range of structure and meter. They drew not only on their own native doggerel (Knittelvers), rhymed couplets, and the simple measures of the anonymous folksong, but imitated very successfully the classical hexameter and Greek free rhythms, Shakespeare's iambic pentameter, the Spanish trochaic tetrameter, and the more exotic and intricate patterns from the Orient, such as the Persian gazel. Despite a marked emphasis on varied form, a striking characteristic of German poetry is its general use of an unpretentious vocabulary. Influenced by the simplicity of the Volkslied, German poets, with a few exceptions such as Stefan George, have generally eschewed an esoteric vocabulary and preferred the words of everyday language, imparting to them new meaning and poetic value. This simplicity has undoubtedly contributed toward making German poetry (together with the theater) one of the art forms closest to the hearts of the people. Its striking popularity dates as far back as the minnesongs and the legendary poetry contests at the Wartburg, portrayed in Wagner's Tannhäuser. In the sixteenth century special schools were established at Nuremberg and Mainz to teach the composition of texts and melodies which, if not always resulting in great poetry, nevertheless continued the tradition of poetry as an art arising directly from the hearts and minds of the people.

Unlike the poetry of many other countries, German poetry was an art form which originated in the grass roots; it was considered not merely a pastime for the more educated. The popular appeal of German poetry is also mirrored in the vital role German poets and their works have played as the voice of a social or political conscience. Poets of all centuries, such as Bürger and Dehmel, called out against social evils; and during the wars against Napoleon, political poetry rallied the

German people to a fight for liberation. Today German high school students are still taught to memorize and recite ballads and poems by Goethe, Schiller, Heine, and others. Innumerable parodies of the masters known by every schoolboy may even suggest that their popularity has occasionally reached the point of diminishing returns.

The poems for the present anthology offer a panorama of the main trends in the development of the poetry of the German-speaking people. The anthology begins with a minnesong of the early Middle Ages and a poem of the seventeenth century; it then focuses on the Age of Goethe (1749-1832). Goethe more than anyone else impressed his stamp on the German lyric by freeing it from all artificial restraints and affectations. Inspired by Goethe and his contemporaries, German poetry was then able to develop according to its own genius and to advance along new lines which eventually led to the period of Expressionism and Post-Expressionism with which this anthology ends.

The brief introductions will help the reader to understand each poet and discover in what ways each one differs from the others; he will find that every poet is an individual, even though the poet belongs to the same literary movement or mainstream as some of his contemporaries.

The prose translations of each poem are literal and make no attempt at literary distinction. Their purpose is to help the reader achieve greater comprehension although an effort was occasionally made to retain the rhythm of the original poem.

Walther von der Vogelweide

(c. 1170-1230)

Walther von der Vogelweide was the most gifted of
the German minnesingers (singers of love) who, like
the troubadours of other lands, wandered from court

to court, singing their songs of veneration and adoration
to the fair noblewomen, both single and married, of
twelfth and thirteenth-century Europe. Lauded as the
"leader of a choir of nightingales" in the *Tristan and
Isolde* of his contemporary Gottfried von Strassburg,
Walther wrote minnesongs which are distinguished by
a delightful blending of love and nature, a remarkable
euphony, and a sincerity transcending that of the con-
vential courtier. He was the first minnesinger to break
with the poetic convention imposed by the feudal code
of courtly love: Walther not only celebrates his patron-
esses or other noblewomen, but also extols the charms
and beauty of lower-born girls. Indeed, in *Unter der
Linde* he even allows his beloved to admit, though
blushingly, that she enjoyed the caresses of her lover.
Walther's range as a poet is further demonstrated by
his scathing political poems directed against papal in-
terference in German affairs.

Walther wrote the poem *Unter der Linde* in the
language of his time, Middle High German. For com-
parison, the first stanza is given here in the original as
well as in modern German.

UNDER DER LINDEN
(In Middle High German)

Under der linden
an der heide
dâ unser zweier bette was,
dâ muget ir vinden
schône beide
gebrochen bluomen unde gras.
Vor dem walde in einem tal
tandaradei!
    schône sanc diu nahtegal.

UNTER DER LINDE

Unter der Linden
Auf der Heide,
Wo mein Liebster bei mir sass,
Da könnt ihr finden
Gebrochen beide
Bunte Blumen und das Gras.
Im nahen Wald mit hellem Schall,
Tandaradei!
Sang so süss die Nachtigall.

Ich kam gegangen
Hin zur Aue,
Da harrte schon mein Liebster dort
Und hat mich empfangen —
Hehre Fraue —
Dass ich bin selig immerfort.
Küsst' er mich wohl auch zur Stund'?
Tandaradei!
Seht, wie rot mir ist der Mund.

Da hat er gemachet
Hurtig voll Freude
Ein Ruheplätzchen für uns zwei.
Darob wird gelachet
Sicher noch heute,
Kommt jemand dort des Wegs vorbei.
An den Rosen er wohl mag —
Tandaradei!
Merken, wo das Haupt mir lag.

UNDER THE LINDEN

Under the linden
On the heath,
Where my sweetheart sat with me,
There you can find
Broken, both
Colorful flowers and grass.
In the nearby woods, with ringing sound
Tandaradei!
So sweetly sang the nightingale.

I came walking
Up to the meadow,
My sweetheart waited there already
And he received me —
Noble Lady —
So that I'm blissful forevermore.
Did he also kiss me then?
Tandaradei!
Look, how red my mouth is.

Then he made,
Nimble with joy,
A small resting-place for the two of us.
They laugh about this
Surely still today
If someone should pass by that way.
From the roses he probably can
Tandaradei!
Tell where my head was lying.

Dass er mich herzte,
Wüsste es einer,
Behüte Gott! so schämte ich mich;
Und wie er scherzte.
Keiner, keiner
Erfahre das als er und ich,
Und das kleine Vögelein —
Tandaradei!
Das wird wohl verschwiegen sein.

That he caressed me,
If someone should know it,
God forbid! I would be ashamed;
And how he joked.
May no one, no one
Learn this but him and me
And that little bird —
Tandaradei!
That will surely be discreet.

Andreas Gryphius
(1616-1664)

German poetry of the seventeenth century, often misunderstood, received scant attention during the nineteenth century. In the twentieth century it was rediscovered, largely through the efforts of the members of the Stefan George circle. (A poem by George also appears in this anthology.) By including many Baroque poems in their collections of poetry and discussing many of the Baroque writers in belletristic magazines and books, these modern poets described and demonstrated the beauty in the poems of their predecessors.

Andreas Gryphius, while never entirely forgotten, also enjoyed a renascence at that time. In many respects he typified the poetry of his age. His choice of the sonnet form for the poem *Menschliches Elende* is characteristic of a period which sought its models in the poets of antiquity and of the Italian Renaissance. But Gryphius and many of his contemporaries poured into the classic forms a content at once so weighty, metaphysical, and anxiety-ridden that it all but burst the measured art form they had chosen.

Gryphius lived in the era of the Thirty Years' War, a time in which in Gryphius' own words:

The towers stand in flames; the church is toppled
down;
The city hall is rubble. The strong have been cut
down,
The virgins have been despoiled. And wherever we
may look
Are fire, pestilence, and death, which pierce through
heart and mind.

The human misery which Gryphius describes is, of course, timeless and immanent. But it is equally true that the sentiment of "all is vanity," discernible in such phrases as "vain dream," and "we perish like smoke," reflected a state of mind peculiar to the emotional climate of the Thirty Years' War.

Another development of the age which had a shattering effect on Western man was the quick progress of the natural sciences. It was now felt that man was but matter, an organism at best. In the poetry of the age man is often compared with concrete physical things; in Gryphius' poem with a residence, a candle, melted snow, etc. These concrete images are not startling in themselves, but coupled as they are with abstract metaphysics, they create tensions within the poem, tensions which are further compounded by the poet's skillful and repeated exploitation of one of the hexameter's inherent characteristics: its proclivity for antithesis. Note how Gryphius loves to use the first six syllables of a line to state a suspense-building premise which, after a tension-filled pause marked by the hexameter's caesura, is then resolved by a foreboding and ominous conclusion contained in the next six syllables.

Simultaneously, the wealth of his imagery sustains interest and the weight of repetition convinces the listener of the poet's utter sincerity. Throughout, we admire Gryphius' facility in inventing new metaphors for human misery. Despite Baroque overstatement and occasional bombast, we are still convinced that the poet is stating the truth of an inner vision. Rent by the disharmony of what is and what ought to be, Gryphius' vision mirrors the age of the Thirty Years' War when civilization and culture almost came to a standstill in Germany. But because of a few such men, ethics and aesthetics continued to live amidst the unleashed forces of bloodshed and violence, disease and destruction.

MENSCHLICHES ELENDE

Was sind wir Menschen doch? Ein Wohnhaus grimmer Schmerzen,
Ein Ball des falschen Glücks, ein Irrlicht dieser Zeit,
Ein Schauplatz herber Angst, besetzt mit scharfem Leid,
Ein bald verschmelzter Schnee und abgebrannte Kerzen.

Dies Leben fleucht davon wie ein Geschwätz und Scherzen.
Die vor uns abgelegt des schwachen Leibes Kleid
Und in das Totenbuch der grossen Sterblichkeit
Längst eingeschrieben sind, sind uns aus Sinn und Herzen.

Gleich wie ein eitel Traum leicht aus der Acht hinfällt
Und wie ein Strom verscheusst, den keine Macht aufhält,
So muss auch unser Nam, Lob, Ehr und Ruhm verschwinden.

Was itzund Atem holt, muss mit der Luft entfliehn,
Was nach uns kommen wird, wird uns ins Grab nachziehn.
Was sag ich? Wir vergehn wie Rauch von*starken Winden.

*In the recording this word was inadvertently read as *vor*.

16

HUMAN MISERY

What, after all, is Man! A dwelling for grim pain,
A mere toy of false fortune, a will-o'-the-wisp of these times,
A stage for bitter fear, replete with cutting grief
A quickly melted snow and a candle soon burned down.

This life flies off like idle talk and jest.
Those who cast off before us the weak body's dress
And into the book of death of great mortality
Have long been inscribed, have vanished from our mind and heart.

Just as a vain dream will lightly be forgotten
And as a stream flows on, which no force can arrest,
So too must disappear our name, praise, honor, fame.

What now is drawing breath, must vanish with the air.
What comes after us, will follow us to the grave.
What say I? We vanish like smoke before strong winds.

Friedrich Gottlieb Klopstock

(1724-1803)

Klopstock's poetry breaks through the playful rococo verses, dry rational poems, and the didactic fables of his predecessors like a fresh spring of genuine feeling. In the decades immediately preceding Klopstock's arrival upon the literary scene, most poets considered poetry a trade, a chore of versifying, in which they "manufactured" *Gelegenheitsgedichte* (poems for the occasion) to gain the favor of the local prince; a trade in which their own emotions were rarely involved. But with the first line of Klopstock's Miltonesque epic, *Der Messias,* the German public of the eighteenth century heard something entirely new; a poet convinced of the dignity of his calling, who introduced daring new images, a more pliant language shorn of artificiality, a free unrhymed rhythmic scheme which liberated German poetry from the shackles of the previous narrow and rigid "rules" about metrics. Equally important, Klopstock reintroduced human passion and religious fervor into its rightful place — lyric poetry. In the simple, serious, soulful and yet non-sensual love-poem *Das Rosenband,* Klopstock also displays his technical ability and inventiveness. The three-line stanza, rather unconventional in itself, is always capped by a climactic third line; the poem enriches the language by such new word formations as *Frühlingsschatten,* and introduces surprising turns of phrase as *doch lispelt ich ihr sprachlos zu.* These and other innovations paved the way for many of Klopstock's successors.

DAS ROSENBAND

Im Frühlingsschatten fand ich sie,
da band ich sie mit Rosenbändern:
sie fühlt es nicht und schlummerte.

Ich sah sie an: mein Leben hing
mit diesem Blick an ihrem Leben:
ich fühlt es wohl und wusst es nicht.

Doch lispelt ich ihr sprachlos zu
und rauschte mit den Rosenbändern:
da wachte sie vom Schlummer auf.

Sie sah mich an, ihr Leben hing
mit diesem Blick an meinem Leben
und um uns wards Elysium.

GARLAND OF ROSES

In the shade of spring I found her,
then with garlands of roses bound her;
she did not feel it and slumbered on.

I looked at her, my life depended
with this one glance upon her life:
I truly felt it, but did not know it.

But speechlessly I whispered to her
and rustled with the rosy garlands:
then she awakened from her slumber.

She looked at me; her life depended
with this one glance upon my life
and around us rose Elysium.

Matthias Claudius
(1740-1815)

Gentle Matthias Claudius, son of a clergyman, planned for several years to follow the calling of his father. Though he never became a pastor, he communicated his deeply felt religious convictions through his essays and poetry. Many of his poems contain the admonitions of a sermon, express Christian compassion, and, like the poem *Mondnacht,* resemble well-known church hymns. This evocation of a literary form with which almost everyone is familiar and the child-like piety which his poems communicate have caused his poems to be included in countless German school readers, beginning with those for the earliest grades.

Editor of various journals and country newspapers, he lived the greater part of his life in small towns and villages where he became deeply rooted in the life around him, so much so that his contemporaries frequently referred to Claudius simply by the name of one of his newspapers, *Der Wandsbecker Bote.* It is therefore scarcely surprising that in his poetry Claudius draws from rural scenes for his metaphors and imagery. In the poem *Abendlied,* as well as in many other of his lyric works, the nature around the poet testifies to God's wisdom and goodness. In this world there is no room for the medieval concept of death, the grim reaper. Claudius sees death as a friend, a belief which was not shaken but fortified by the premature death of his brother and his own critical illness. He calls death *Freund Hein,* a euphemism which has since entered the German language. In the poem *Der Tod und das Mädchen* he states his view of death in the simplest terms, drawing directly upon the language of the common people with words like *Knochenmann* and phrases like *sei gutes Muts.* The contrast between the frantic outcry of the girl and the soothing speech of death, artistically expressed by the short lines of the first stanza and the long-voweled lines of the second, respectively, has been underlined by the musical setting which Schubert created for this poem.

DER TOD UND DAS MÄDCHEN

Das Mädchen:

Vorüber, ach vorüber
geh, wilder Knochenmann!
Ich bin noch jung! Geh, Lieber,
und rühre mich nicht an!

Der Tod:

Gib deine Hand, du schön und zart Gebild!
Bin Freund und komme nicht zu strafen.
Sei gutes Muts! Ich bin nicht wild!
Sollst sanft in meinen Armen schlafen!

ABENDLIED

Der Mond ist aufgegangen,
die goldnen Sternlein prangen
am Himmel hell und klar;
der Wald steht schwarz und schweiget,
und aus den Wiesen steiget
der weisse Nebel wunderbar.

Wie ist die Welt so stille
und in der Dämmrung Hülle
so traulich und so hold!
Als eine stille Kammer,
wo ihr des Tages Jammer
verschlafen und vergessen sollt.

DEATH AND THE MAIDEN

The Maiden:

Go past, oh, go past,
you wild skeleton!
I am still young! Go, dear one,
and do not touch me!

Death:

Give me your hand, you beautiful and tender shape!
I am a friend and do not come to punish.
Be of good cheer! I am not wild!
You shall sleep softly in my arms!

EVENING SONG

The moon has risen,
the golden starlets sparkle
brightly and clearly in the heavens;
the wood stands black and silent
and from the meadows rises
the white fog wondrously.

Oh, how quiet is the world
and in the veil of twilight
so cozy and so lovely!
Just like a peaceful chamber
where the sorrow of the day
you shall forget and sleep away.

Seht ihr den Mond dort stehen?
Er ist nur halb zu sehen,
und ist doch rund und schön!
So sind wohl manche Sachen,
die wir getrost belachen,
weil unsre Augen sie nicht sehn.

Wir stolze Menschenkinder
sind eitel arme Sünder,
und wissen gar nicht viel;
wir spinnen Luftgespinste
und suchen viele Künste
und kommen weiter von dem Ziel.

Gott, lass uns *dein Heil* schauen,
auf nichts Vergänglichs trauen,
nicht Eitelkeit uns freun!
Lass uns einfältig werden,
und vor dir hier auf Erden
wie Kinder fromm und fröhlich sein!

Wollst endlich sonder Grämen
aus dieser Welt uns nehmen
durch einen sanften Tod,
und, wenn du uns genommen,
lass uns in Himmel kommen,
du unser Herr und unser Gott!

So legt euch denn, ihr Brüder,
in Gottes Namen nieder!
Kalt ist der Abendhauch.
Verschon uns, Gott! mit Strafen,
und lass uns ruhig schlafen,
und unsern kranken Nachbar auch!

The moon, you see it stand there?
You can see but half of it
and yet it's round and beautiful.
So are so many things,
which we presume to laugh at,
because our eyes don't see them.

We proud sons of men
are nothing but poor sinners
and know not much at all;
we are spinning idle daydreams
and search for many arts
and get but farther from our goal.

God, let us perceive your grace,
not trust in passing things,
not glory in conceit!
Allow us to grow guileless,
and before Thee here on earth
be like children, devout and gay.

And, last, without affliction,
Take us from this earth
by means of gentle death,
And when Thou hast removed us,
let us get into heaven,
Thou our Lord and God.

So lie down then, brothers,
in the name of God!
The breath of eve is cool.
Spare us, oh Lord, from punishment
and let us sleep in peace
and our sick neighbor, too.

Gottfried August Bürger
(1747-1794)

The life of Gottfried August Bürger was rent by constant privation, professional crises, and emotional turmoil. Up to the year of his death he was forced to supplement his sparse income by literary hack work and except for a brief career as professor of literature at the University of Göttingen, he held a series of positions which, he felt, all but smothered his creative abilities. His three marriages all ended catastrophically. After marrying Dorette Leonhart, he found himself equally in love with his wife's sister, the Molly of his poetry. For nearly ten years, he maintained an unconventional household with both sisters, and then both died within a year and a half; first Dorette and then Molly, whom he had married upon the death of her sister. His brief third marriage ended in divorce. But out of his troubles were born several volumes of poetry which had already earned him during his lifetime the title of "the people's poet." By linking his poems to contemporary events and issues and by striking a consistently popular note, in the best sense of the phrase, he reached a wide and diversified audience. His lengthy ballad *Lenore* gained world-wide recognition and became a literary manifesto of the Age of Romanticism; his political essays have been called battle-songs against absolutism. His poem *Der Bauer— An seinen Durchlauchtigen Tyrannen,* which attacks the abuses of Germany's petty tyrants with even greater force and conviction than his essays, is equally deserving of this label.

DER BAUER

An seinen Durchlauchtigen Tyrannen

Wer bist du, Fürst, dass ohne Scheu
Zerrollen mich dein Wagenrad,
Zerschlagen darf dein Ross?

Wer bist du, Fürst, dass in mein Fleisch
Dein Freund, dein Jagdhund, ungebleut
Darf Klau' und Rachen hau'n?

Wer bist du, dass, durch Saat und Forst,
Das Hurra deiner Jagd mich treibt,
Entatmet wie das Wild? —

Die Saat, so deine Jagd zertritt,
Was Ross, und Hund, und du verschlingst,
Das Brot, du Fürst, ist mein.

Du Fürst hast nicht, bei Egg' und Pflug,
Hast nicht den Erntetag durchschwitzt.
Mein, mein ist Fleiss und Brot! —

Ha! du wärst Obrigkeit von Gott?
Gott spendet Segen aus; du raubst!
Du nicht von Gott, Tyrann!

THE PEASANT

To His Gracious Tyrant

Who are you, Prince, that without fear,
Your wagon wheel may crush me,
Your horse may dash me down?

Who are you, Prince, that into my flesh
Your friend, your hunting-dog, unwhipped,
May sink his claws and jaw?

Who are you, that through crops and woods,
The yelling of your hunt will drive me,
Panting like the game?—

The crop that's trampled by your hunt,
What horse and dog and you devour,
The bread, Prince, is mine.

You, Prince, did not, with harrow and plow,
Sweat through the day of harvest.
The effort and the bread are mine! —

Ha! You claim authority from God?
God hands out blessings; you but rob!
You are not sent by God, tyrant!

Ludwig Heinrich Christoph Hölty
(1748-1776)

The staid University of Göttingen became a literary center from approximately 1770 to 1775, including among its members a remarkably large number of students with a gift for poetry. Prompted in part by the enterprise of two undergraduates, who founded a literary magazine, and encouraged by the blessings of Klopstock, then Germany's foremost poet, these young men united in a literary society, *Der Göttinger Hain*. Here they set poetic tasks for one another and read and criticized each other's work. The poems resulting from this cross-fertilization of ideas were frequently of lasting quality. This holds especially true for the poems of Ludwig Hölty, a student of theology, who lived only a short time after his university years. His poems often reflect his understanding and love of nature; just as frequently they strike a note of impending death. In this poem both themes are clearly discernible; the images are taken from nature, while early death strikes down both the young boy and the bride. But from this vision of death Hölty draws not melancholy but rather an affirmation of life. If death is inevitable, let us seize the day and taste to the full the joys of nature, love, and wine. This sentiment of *carpe diem* unites Hölty with such poets as Herrick "Gather ye rosebuds," Marvell "To his coy mistress," Marlowe "Come live with me" and Ronsard *"A la belle Hélène."*

33

LEBENSPFLICHTEN

Rosen auf den Weg gestreut,
und des Harms vergessen!
Eine kleine Spanne Zeit
ward uns zugemessen.

Heute hüpft im Frühlingstanz
noch der frohe Knabe;
morgen weht der Totenkranz
schon auf seinem Grabe.

Wonne führt die junge Braut
heute zum Altare;
eh die Abendwolke taut
ruht sie auf der Bahre.

Ungewisser, kurzer Dau'r
ist dies Erdenleben
und zur Freude, nicht zur Trau'r
uns von Gott gegeben.

Gebet Harm und Grillenfang,
gebet ihn den Winden;
ruht bei frohem Becherklang
unter grünen Linden!

Lasset keine Nachtigall
unbehorcht verstummen,
keine Bien' im Frühlingstal
unbelauschet summen.

Fühlt, solang, es Gott erlaubt,
Kuss und süsse Trauben,
bis der Tod, der alles raubt,
kommt, sie euch zu rauben.

DUTIES OF LIFE

Let's strew roses upon our path,
let's forget our sorrow!
Just a little span of time
has been measured out to us.

Today the happy boy still leaps
in the dance of springtime;
tomorrow the wreath of death
already flutters on his grave.

Today joy leads on the youthful bride
stepping to the altar;
before the evening's cloud dissolves
she rests on her bier.

Of uncertain, short duration
is this life on earth
and for enjoyment, not for sadness
given us by God.

Give your sorrow and caprice,
give it to the winds;
rest while happy cups resound
under the green lindens!

Let no single nightingale
end her song unheard,
nor a bee in springtime's vale
hum without your listening.

Taste, as long as God will grant
kisses and sweet grapes,
until death, which steals everything,
comes to steal them from you.

Unser schlummerndes Gebein,
in die Gruft gesäet,
fühlet nicht den Rosenhain,
der das Grab umwehet;

Fühlet nicht den Wonneklang
angestossner Becher,
nicht den frohen Rundgesang
weingelehrter Zecher.*

*In the recording this line was inadvertently read as *weinbelaubter Zecher.*

Our slumbering bones,
sown into the tomb,
do not feel the grove of roses
which flutters round our grave;

Do not feel the sound of joy
of cups clinking together,
nor the happy roundelay
of carousers, made wise by wine.

Johann Wolfgang von Goethe
(1749-1832)

Goethe was Germany's greatest lyric poet, a unique genius, who excelled in every lyric genre he attempted. His collection of poetry runs the gamut from the Anacreontic poems of wine, women, and song to the ballad, from pure nature lyrics to biting satiric epigrams, from philosophic-rationalistic poems to irrational outbursts of pure emotion, from the simple form of the folk song to sonnets, from poems in seemingly artless doggerel to those imitating elaborate Greek, Spanish, and Oriental verse forms. And this enumeration is by no means a complete catalogue of his poetic creations. The poems printed below, written at three different stages of his development as a lyric poet, give but a bare hint of his versatility. The first one, *Gesang der Geister über den Wassern,* was written during his early period of Storm-and-Stress, when his poems swept away the older tradition of rationalistic and conventional poetry by their spontaneity, emotional power, intense empathy with nature, and instinctive feeling for the right form. This poem reflects one further dimension of his early poetry: his ability to express his views of life by symbols taken from nature. Goethe wrote this poem after observing an Alpine brook cascading downward; the flow of the brook becomes the symbol of human life which to Goethe is but a part of a pantheistic universe. In describing the wind, the symbol for human fate, as "the beautiful wooer," he displays a joyful acceptance of the fact that Man, like the brook, must rise and fall between heaven and earth, must meet opposition — but may also serve as a mirror to the stars.

The second poem was written during Goethe's classical period, after he had returned from Italy. Here, as in many poems written during this stage of his development, Goethe imposes a more stringent, "classical" form on his poems; the content becomes more Greek and Roman in theme, and his outlook on life more pagan. Goethe wrote the *Roman Elegies,* of which the fifth is reprinted, in distichs, a two-line verse form in which a line of hexameter is followed by a line of pentameter. The meter, the references to Roman gods and to Roman love poets — who were not yet troubled by the Christian dichotomy of flesh *versus* soul — all testify to Goethe's profound immersion in the world of antiquity.

In his late poems, Goethe worked with innumerable forms of world literature, reverting occasionally to the style of his earliest poetry, in which he attempted to capture the simple language and unsophisticated structure of folk poetry. *Gefunden* has all these characteristics; its uncomplicated symbolism is likewise reminiscent of the *Volkslied.* To understand fully this delightful short poem, one need only know that here Goethe retells, symbolically, his relationship to his wife Christiane.

GESANG DER GEISTER
ÜBER DEN WASSERN

Des Menschen Seele
Gleicht dem Wasser:
Vom Himmel kommt es,
Zum Himmel steigt es,
Und wieder nieder
Zur Erde muss es,
Ewig wechselnd.

Strömt von der hohen,
Steilen Felswand
Der reine Strahl,
Dann stäubt er lieblich
In Wolkenwellen
Zum glatten Fels,
Und leicht empfangen
Wallt er verschleiernd,
Leisrauschend
Zur Tiefe nieder.

Ragen Klippen
Dem Sturz entgegen,
Schäumt er unmutig
Stufenweise
Zum Abgrund.

Im flachen Bette
Schleicht er das Wiesental hin,
Und in dem glatten See
Weiden ihr Antlitz
Alle Gestirne.

SONG OF THE SPIRITS
OVER THE WATERS

Man's soul
Equals the water:
From Heaven it comes,
To Heaven it rises,
And downward again
It must descend to the earth,
Forever changing.

When there streams from the high,
Steep wall of the rock
The pure jet of water,
Then it foams in lovely sprays
In waves of clouds
To the smooth rock,
And gracefully received,
It floats, enveiling,
Murmuring softly
Down to the deep.

Where cliffs arise
In the face of the downpour,
It foams, out of temper,
Step upon step,
Down to the abyss.

In the shallow bed
It creeps down the meadowy valley
And in the smooth lake
Their countenance feast
All heavenly bodies.

Wind ist der Welle
Lieblicher Buhler;
Wind mischt vom Grund aus
Schäumende Wogen.

Seele des Menschen,
Wie gleichst du dem Wasser!
Schicksal des Menschen,
Wie gleichst du dem Wind!

The wind is the wave's
Beautiful wooer;
The wind stirs up from the bottom
Foaming waves.

Soul of Man,
How you resemble the water!
Fate of Man,
How you resemble the wind!

From RÖMISCHE ELEGIEN

Froh empfind ich mich nun auf klassischem Boden
   begeistert,
Vor- und Mitwelt spricht lauter und reizender mir.
Hier befolg' ich den Rat, durchblättre die Werke der
   Alten
Mit geschäftiger Hand, täglich mit neuem Genuss.
Aber die Nächte hindurch hält Amor mich anders
   beschäftigt;
Werd' ich auch halb nur gelehrt, bin ich doch doppelt
   beglückt.
Und belehr' ich mich nicht, indem ich des lieblichen
   Busens
Formen spähe, die Hand leite die Hüften hinab?
Dann versteh ich den Marmor erst recht: ich
   denk und vergleiche,
Sehe mit fühlendem Aug, fühle mit sehender Hand.
Raubt die Liebste denn gleich mir einige Stunden des
   Tages,
Gibt sie Stunden der Nacht mir zur Entschädigung hin.
Wird doch nicht immer geküsst, es wird vernünftig
   gesprochen;
Überfällt sie der Schlaf, lieg' ich und denke mir
   viel.
Oftmals hab' ich auch schon in ihren Armen gedichtet
Und des Hexameters Mass leise mit fingernder
   Hand
Ihr auf den Rücken gezählt. Sie atmet in lieblichem
   Schlummer,
Und es durchglühet ihr Hauch mir bis ins Tiefste
   die Brust.
Amor schüret die Lamp' indes und denket der Zeiten,
Da er den nämlichen Dienst seinen Triumvirn getan.

From *ROMAN ELEGIES*

Joyously I find myself enraptured on classical soil;
Times past and present speak louder and more
   delightfully to me.
Here I follow the counsel, leaf through the works of
   the ancients
With industrious hand, daily with pleasure renewed.
But throughout the night Amor otherwise keeps me
   busy;
Even though only half enlightened, I am doubly made
   happy.
And am I not learning, when the beauteous
   bosom's
Form I seek out, my hand descends on her hips?
Then I comprehend, truly, the marble; I think
   and compare,
See with feeling eye, feel with seeing hand.
Though the beloved robs me of some hours of
   daytime,
She gives me hours of night in compensation.
After all, we do not kiss all the time, there is also sensible
   discourse;
When sleep overcomes her, I lie and think
   much.
Ofttimes in her arms I even wrote poems
And, with fingering hand, the hexameter's
   measure
I counted out on her back. She breathes in loveliest
   slumber,
And her breath glows into the deepest parts of my
   breast.
Amor, meanwhile, stirs up the lamp-light and remembers
   the era
When for his triumvirs he did the like service.

45

GEFUNDEN

Ich ging im Walde
So für mich hin,
Und nichts zu suchen,
Das war mein Sinn.

Im Schatten sah ich
Ein Blümchen stehn,
Wie Sterne leuchtend,
Wie Äuglein schön.

Ich wollt' es brechen,
Da sagt' es fein:
Soll ich zum Welken
Gebrochen sein?

Ich grub's mit allen
Den Würzlein aus,
Zum Garten trug ich's
Am hübschen Haus.

Und pflanzt' es wieder
Am stillen Ort;
Nun zweigt es immer
Und blüht so fort.

FOUND

I walked in the forest
So all by myself,
And to search for nothing
That was my intent.

In the shadow I saw
A small flower standing,
Shining like stars,
Beautiful as tender eyes.

I wanted to pluck it,
When it delicately said:
Shall I to wither
Be broken off?

I dug it up with all
Its small roots,
To the garden I brought it
By the pretty house.

And once more did plant it
At a quiet nook;
Now it branches forever
And continues to bloom.

Jakob Michael Reinhold Lenz
(1751-1792)

The life of the poet Lenz is in many ways characteristic of the young generation of poets of the Storm-and-Stress era. Like most members of this group Lenz revolted against rationalistic sobriety, traditional literary forms, and wrote frankly emotional works which despite frequent formlessness are intensely powerful. After five years of burning literary activity his creative genius-like talent gradually ebbed away during repeated onsets of mental disturbances.

Lenz both profited and suffered from his contacts with Goethe. In his adulation of Goethe, Lenz emulated his life and works to such an extent that the Duke of Weimar nicknamed him *Goethes Affe* (Goethe's ape or mimic). Yet by imitating Goethe, Lenz occasionally produced poems which came so close to Goethe's style and lyric gift, that for a long time they were incorrectly attributed to the master. In the case of the poem below there was an added reason for this belief. Lenz presented this poem to Friederike Brion, an Alsatian parson's daughter with whom he had fallen in love — the identical girl who had inspired some of Goethe's most fervent love lyrics in the previous year. *Wo bist du itzt,* in which Lenz deplores his temporary separation from Friederike, displays the simplicity, spontaneity, and personal note of Goethe's early poetry; it also contains a device characteristic of Lenz' style: the repetition of words and phrases (the *wo* of the first stanza, the *komm zurück* of the last). These repetitions heighten the poetic effect; here they help to evoke a mood of sadness which envelops the author, heaven, and earth.

In recent years the life and works of Lenz have again been brought to the attention of a wider public. The German poet and theater director Bertolt Brecht staged several of Lenz' dramas and the *Partisan Review* published a translation of Georg Büchner's short novel *Lenz* which gives insight into the tortured mind of the poet.

"WO BIST DU ITZT"

Wo bist du itzt, mein unvergesslich Mädchen,
Wo singst du itzt?
Wo lacht die Flur, wo triumphiert das Städtchen,
Das dich besitzt?

Seit du entfernt, will keine Sonne scheinen,
Und es vereint
Der Himmel sich, dir zärtlich nachzuweinen,
Mit deinem Freund.

All unsre Lust ist fort mit dir gezogen,
Still überall
Ist Stadt und Feld. Dir nach ist sie geflogen,
Die Nachtigall.

O komm zurück! Schon rufen Hirt und Herden
Dich bang herbei.
Komm bald zurück! Sonst wird es Winter werden
Im Monat Mai.

"WHERE ARE YOU NOW"

Where are you now, my unforgettable maiden,
Where do you sing now?
Where smiles the field, where does the small town triumph
Which possesses you?

Since you are gone, no sun will shine
And Heaven itself,
To weep after you tenderly,
Unites with your friend.

All our happiness has gone with you,
Quiet everywhere
Is town and field. It followed you in flight —
The nightingale.

Oh do return! Already herds and shepherds
Recall you anxiously.
Oh, come back soon! Else there will be winter
In the month of May.

Friedrich Schiller
(1759-1805)

Schiller, often extolled as Germany's foremost dramatic author, carried his flair for dramatic presentation into his lyric poems. Since the ballad is the most dramatic form in poetry, it is scarcely surprising that Schiller was inevitably drawn to this form and produced many of his most popular poems in it. With the ballad *Der Handschuh* we can gain insight into his lyric-dramatic workshop, especially since the source of the poem, a less-than-hundred word anecdote, has come down to us. Out of this sparse raw material Schiller wove the strands of his ballad, instinctively using the methods of the theater. In the first stanza Schiller sets his stage; the second, third, and fourth stanza resemble the "rising action" of the drama, provided in the poem by the ever more exciting appearance of the ferocious animals. Here Schiller has transformed the static description of an anecdote into gripping, dynamic action. The climax comes with the mocking challenge of the frivolous damsel and the knight's descent into the dangerous arena. The final stanza, like the last act of a play, brings the terse and surprising solution.

Schiller's ballads, in contrast to the ordinary folk-ballads, usually contain a philosophical, ethical, or moral idea. When Schiller called this poem a *Nach-stück* (epilogue) to his earlier ballad, "The Diver," he provided a clue to the idea underlying *Der Hand-schuh*. With both poems comes the admonition that "Man must not tempt the gods." But while the solution in the earlier work is tragic, here Schiller drives the lesson home with a twist not devoid of grim humor.

DER HANDSCHUH

Vor seinem Löwengarten,
das Kampfspiel zu erwarten,
sass König Franz,
und um ihn die Grossen der Krone,
und rings auf hohem Balkone
die Damen in schönem Kranz.

Und wie er winkt mit dem Finger
auftut sich der weite Zwinger:
und hinein mit bedächtigem Schritt
ein Löwe tritt
und sieht sich stumm
rings um,
mit langem Gähnen,
und schüttelt die Mähnen,
und streckt die Glieder,
und legt sich nieder.

Und der König winkt wieder,
da öffnet sich behend
ein zweites Tor,
daraus rennt
mit wildem Sprunge
ein Tiger hervor.
Wie er den Löwen erschaut,
brüllt er laut,
schlägt mit dem Schweif
einen furchtbaren Reif,
und recket die Zunge,
und im Kreise scheu
umgeht er den Leu,
grimmig schnurrend;
drauf streckt er sich murrend
zur Seite nieder.

THE GLOVE

Before his lions' arena
awaiting the contest
sat King Francis
and, around him, the grandees of the realm
and all around on the high balcony
the ladies in beautiful array.

And when he beckons with his finger
the wide arena opens
and into it with deliberate stride
steps a lion
and silently looks
all around,
with a drawn-out yawn
and shakes his mane
and stretches his limbs
and lies down.

And the king beckons again,
thereupon opens quickly
a second gate
out of which runs
with a wild jump
a tiger.
When he catches sight of the lion
he roars loudly,
describes with his tail
a horrifying circle,
and extends his tongue,
and circling warily
he walks around the lion,
purring grimly;
then growling he lies down
at the side.

Und der König winkt wieder,
da speit das doppelt geöffnete Haus
zwei Leoparden auf einmal aus,
die stürzen mit mutiger Kampfbegier
auf das Tigertier;
das packt sie mit seinen grimmigen Tatzen,
und der Leu mit Gebrüll
richtet sich auf—da wird's still;
und herum im Kreis,
von Mordsucht heiss,
lagern sich die greulichen Katzen.

Da fällt von des Altans Rand
ein Handschuh von schöner Hand
zwischen den Tiger und den Leun
mitten hinein.

Und zu Ritter Delorges, spottenderweis',
wendet sich Fräulein Kunigund:
"Herr Ritter, ist Eure Lieb' so heiss,
wie Ihr mir's schwört zu jeder Stund,
ei, so hebt mir den Handschuh auf!"

Und der Ritter in schnellem Lauf,
steigt hinab in den furchtbaren Zwinger
mit festem Schritte,
und aus der Ungeheuer Mitte
nimmt er den Handschuh mit keckem Finger.

Und mit Erstaunen und mit Grauen
sehen's die Ritter und Edelfrauen,
und gelassen bringt er den Handschuh zurück.
Da schallt ihm sein Lob aus jedem Munde,
Aber mit zärtlichem Liebesblick —
er verheisst ihm sein nahes Glück —
empfängt ihn Fräulein Kunigunde.
Und er wirft ihr den Handschuh ins Gesicht:
"Den Dank, Dame, begehr ich nicht!"
Und verlässt sie zur selben Stunde.

And the king beckons again,
thereupon the house, both gates unlocked, discharges
two leopards, both at once,
which rush with courageous pugnacity
toward the tiger;
he seizes them with his grim paws,
and the lion, with a roar,
arises—then it becomes quiet;
and around in a circle,
burning from the passion to murder
the dreadful cats crouch down.

Then there falls from the balcony
a glove from a beautiful hand
between the tiger and the lion
right between them.

And to the Knight Delorges, mockingly,
turns Damsel Kunigund:
"My knight, if your love is so ardent,
as you swear to me at all hours,
well then, pick up my glove!"

And the knight in a quick run,
descends into the horrible arena,
with firm step,
and from the midst of the monsters
he takes the glove with bold fingers.

And with astonishment and a shudder
the knights and the noblewomen watch,
and calmly he brings back the glove.
Now praise resounds for him from every mouth;
But with a tender glance of love —
it promises him his approaching happiness —
Damsel Kunigund receives him.
And he throws the glove into her face:
"Your gratitude, milady, I do not desire!"
And he leaves her at the selfsame hour.

Friedrich Hölderlin
(1770-1843)

Hyperion, the hero of Hölderlin's novel about Greece's heroic struggle against Turkey, intones this song after the cause of Greek liberty is lost and his beloved, Diotima, Hölderlin's vision of Hellenic perfection, has died. But "Hyperion's Song of Destiny" is also the pathetic expression of Hölderlin's own tragic fate. The tumbling water, which in the poem is hurled from precipice to precipice, also symbolizes how the poet himself was preoccupied with an uncertain future. Abandoning his initial occupation as a private tutor, which he disliked thoroughly, Hölderlin wandered restlessly about in Switzerland and Southern France and in 1802 returned mentally ill to his home in Swabia. An improvement in his condition enabled him to work briefly as a librarian — but in 1806 he had a relapse and spent the remaining thirty-seven years of his life in total mental darkness, first in an asylum, then in the house of a kindly carpenter in Tübingen near his hometown on the river Neckar.

Hölderlin's poems seem to capture the very spirit of Hellenism; the ones written in classical or free verse forms on Greek themes represent the poet at his best. Hölderlin, however, did not see ancient Greece as Winckelmann or Goethe had seen it: calm, sublimated, classic, Apollonian. Anticipating Nietzsche, Hölderlin no longer deified Greek culture for its "noble simplicity and quiet grandeur;" to him Greek culture was irrational and emotional, an outburst of elemental forces dominated by Dionysos, the god of ecstasy and bacchanalian orgies. Like "Hyperion's Song of Destiny" most of Hölderlin's poems reflect his passionate yearning for a harmony he never attained; his verse is the outpouring of the god-inspired poet filled with poetic frenzy. Although the language and meaning of his poems are often difficult to penetrate and will always remain a stumbling block to some readers, he has appealed with ever-increasing force to our generation and in the last decades has come to be recognized as one of the world's great lyric poets.

HYPERIONS SCHICKSALSLIED

Ihr wandelt droben im Licht
auf weichem Boden, selige Genien!
Glänzende Götterlüfte
rühren euch leicht,
wie die Finger der Künstlerin
heilige Saiten.

Schicksallos, wie der schlafende
Säugling, atmen die Himmlischen;
keusch bewahrt
in bescheidener Knospe,
blühet ewig
ihnen der Geist;
und die seligen Augen
blicken in stiller
ewiger Klarheit.

Doch uns ist gegeben
auf keiner Stätte zu ruhn;
es schwinden, es fallen
die leidenden Menschen
blindlings von einer
Stunde zur andern,
wie Wasser von Klippe
zu Klippe geworfen,
jahrlang ins Ungewisse hinab.

HYPERION'S SONG OF DESTINY

You stride up there in the light
on soft ground, blessed spirits!
Luminous divine breezes
touch you gently,
as the fingers of a woman player
touch holy strings.

Freed of all fate, as the sleeping
infant, breathe those in heaven:
chastely preserved
in a modest bud,
their spirit
blossoms eternally;
and their blessed eyes
look out in peaceful,
perpetual clearness.

But to us has been allotted
to rest at no abode;
vanish and fall
will a suffering mankind
blindly from one
hour unto the next,
be cast like the water
from cliff unto cliff,
through the years, down into the uncertain.

Friedrich von Hardenberg (Novalis)

(1772-1801)

Novalis, the pseudonym by which the poet is generally known, was the outstanding lyric genius of the early German Romantic movement. He created the Blue Flower as the symbol of romantic longing — the color blue standing for the infinity of the sky. Paradoxically enough he was both a mining engineer and a religious mystic, an efficient business man and the most visionary of poets.

Novalis' poetic genius was aroused to fervid intensity by the death of his bride, Sophie von Kühn, to whom he had become engaged when she was barely thirteen, and who died shortly after her fifteenth birthday. From his deeply felt grief and an occult death-wish sprang his *Hymnen an die Nacht,* a lyric cycle, to some extent influenced by Young's *Night Thoughts.* Despite Novalis' sorrow, the *Hymns to the Night* (and here night is a symbol for death) are no lamentation. Instead all the poems in the cycle, including the one quoted, express the poet's intense desire to follow his beloved into death, for death frees all mortals from their unrequited longings. Death is the ultimate reality, the reunion with the Infinite, with God. But to Novalis, Death also becomes an erotic fulfilment, a sensual longing beautifully expressed by the sensuous flow and liquid quality of his verse.

Novalis' death-wish was soon to be granted; he died of consumption at the age of twenty-eight, four years after Sophie.

From HYMNEN AN DIE NACHT

Hinüber wall ich,
Und jede Pein
Wird einst ein Stachel
Der Wollust sein.
Noch wenig Zeiten,
So bin ich los,
Und liege trunken
Der Lieb im Schoss.
Unendliches Leben
Wogt mächtig in mir,
Ich schaue von oben
Herunter nach dir.
An jenem Hügel
Verlischt dein Glanz—
Ein Schatten bringet
Den kühlenden Kranz.
O! sauge, Geliebter,
Gewaltig mich an,
Dass ich entschlummern
Und lieben kann.
Ich fühle des Todes
Verjüngende Flut,
Zu Balsam und Äther
Verwandelt mein Blut —
Ich lebe bei Tage
Voll Glauben und Mut
Und sterbe die Nächte
In heiliger Glut.

From *HYMNS TO THE NIGHT*

I'm wandering across,
And every pain
Will someday a sting
Of blissfulness be.
Just a little more time
And I shall be free
And drunkenly lie
In the lap of my love.
Infinite life
Swells mighty in me,
I look from above
Down after you.
At yonder hillside
Your glow becomes dim —
A shadow is bringing
The cooling wreath.
Oh! draw me, beloved,
With force unto you,
That I may fall into slumber
And be able to love.
I feel death's
Rejuvenating flood,
Into balsam and aether
My blood being transformed —
I live through the day
Full of courage and faith
And die in the nights
In holy fire.

Joseph Freiherr von Eichendorff
(1788-1857)

The Silesian Eichendorff was a member of the later Romantic School. Its mouthpiece, the *Zeitung für Einsiedler (Journal for Hermits)*, was published in Heidelberg. This citadel of poetic glamour with its lovely surroundings taught him wherein his talent lay: seeing and hearing God in all nature. Most of his serene and melodious lyrics are inspired by this devout love of God's world, especially by his empathy with the magic beauty of moonlit meadows, fields, valleys, mountains, and forests. They reflect his special gift for expressing with a simple piety akin to that of Francis of Assisi his childlike faith and delight in nature as the living evidence and the very embodiment of divine Providence. Like no other poet, Eichendorff glorified romantic *Wanderlust* and *Heimweh* (homesickness); he was convinced that the joys of wandering were God's special gift to mankind. In his poem *Mondnacht,* as in so many of his nature lyrics, he transmutes nature's visible beauty into an audible one. He felt that the melody of Nature's symphony — such as the gentle rustling of the woods or the murmur of a brook — becomes more audible at night or dusk, when all the noises of civilization are muted. Inspired by the flowing musicality of his verses, many great masters of the German art song have set them to music — foremost among more than 1700 compositions to Eichendorff's poems is Robert Schumann's *Liederkreis,* one of the composer's best known works in this art form. Eichendorff also gained international fame as the author of *Aus dem Leben eines Taugenichts,* a short novel in praise of *dolce far niente,* vagabondage, and the happy-go-lucky life.

MONDNACHT

Es war, als hätt' der Himmel
Die Erde still geküsst,
Dass sie im Blütenschimmer
Von ihm nun träumen müsst'.

Die Luft ging durch die Felder,
Die Ähren wogten sacht,
Es rauschten leis die Wälder,
So sternklar war die Nacht.

Und meine Seele spannte
Weit ihre Flügel aus,
Flog durch die stillen Lande,
Als flöge sie nach Haus.

MOONLIT NIGHT

It was as if Heaven
Had quietly kissed the earth,
Which now, in blossom's glimmer,
Had to dream of him.

The breeze went through the fields,
The ears of grain surged softly,
The forests rustled gently,
The night was so star-bright.

And my soul extended
Its wings so wide,
It flew through the quiet regions
As though it were flying home.

Adalbert von Chamisso
(1781-1838)

Louis Charles Adelaide de Chamisso was eight years old when his family fled from the terror of the French Revolution and settled in Berlin. Although Chamisso wavered for a while between German and his native French as his poetic medium, his German poems rarely betray his French origin. Most of his poems are taken from German legend and story, and some of his ballads are so remarkably German in mood and expression that they have become true folk ballads. Others deal eloquently with the social and political questions of his day. Despite the fact that Chamisso was a victim of the revolutionary upheaval, his poems, such as *Das Riesenspielzeug* (The Giant's Toy) or *Der Bettler und sein Hund* (The Beggar and His Dog), express sympathy for the common people and the need for social reform. *Das Schloss Boncourt* is one of the rare poems alluding directly to his past. Here nostalgic remembrance of his ancestral castle, destroyed in the Revolution, is ultimately absorbed by a deep love for France and the French people.

Chamisso's continuing stature as a poet is assured by his *Frauenliebe und -leben,* immortalized by Robert Schumann, and by his delightful novella *Peter Schlemihl,* the story of the hapless fellow who sold his shadow to the devil for a bottomless purse.

DAS SCHLOSS BONCOURT

Ich träum' als Kind mich zurücke
Und schüttle mein greises Haupt;
Wie sucht ihr mich heim, ihr Bilder,
Die lang ich vergessen geglaubt!

Hoch ragt aus schatt'gen Gehegen
Ein schimmerndes Schloss hervor;
Ich kenne die Türme, die Zinnen,
Die steinerne Brücke, das Tor.

Es schauen vom Wappenschilde
Die Löwen so traulich mich an;
Ich grüsse die alten Bekannten
Und eile den Burghof hinan.

Dort liegt die Sphinx am Brunnen,
Dort grünt der Feigenbaum,
Dort, hinter diesen Fenstern,
Verträumt' ich den ersten Traum.

Ich tret' in die Burgkapelle
Und suche des Ahnherrn Grab;
Dort ist's, dort hängt vom Pfeiler
Das alte Gewaffen herab.

Noch lesen umflort die Augen
Die Züge der Inschrift nicht,
Wie hell durch die bunten Scheiben
Das Licht darüber auch bricht.

So stehst du, o Schloss meiner Väter,
Mir treu und fest in dem Sinn,
Und bist von der Erde verschwunden,
Der Pflug geht über dich hin.

THE CASTLE BONCOURT

I dream of myself in my childhood
And I shake my greying head,
How you do haunt me, you visions,
Which I believed forgotten for long.

There towers above shady woodlands
A glimmering castle so high;
I know the towers, the battlements,
The bridge of stone, the gate.

From the escutcheon there gaze
The lions so familiarly at me;
I greet the old acquaintances
And rush upward over the courtyard.

There the sphinx lies at the fountain,
There the fig-tree is getting green,
There behind these windows,
I dreamt away my first dream.

I step into the castle's chapel
And search for my ancestor's grave;
There it is, there hangs down from the pillar
The olden collection of arms.

My eyes, dimmed with tears, do not read yet
The lines of the inscription,
No matter how brightly, through the colored panes,
The light shines on them.

Thus you stand, castle of my fathers,
Faithful and firm in my mind,
And you have disappeared from the earth,
The plow passes over you.

Sei fruchtbar, o teurer Boden!
Ich segne dich mild und gerührt
Und segn' ihn zwiefach, wer immer
Den Pflug nun über dich führt.

Ich aber will auf mich raffen,
Mein Saitenspiel in der Hand,
Die Weiten der Erde durchschweifen
Und singen von Land zu Land.

Be fertile, oh beloved soil!
I bless you, gently and moved,
And twice I bless whoever
Now leads the plow over you.

But I will arouse myself,
With my lyre held in my hand
And roam the breadth of the earth
And sing from land to land.

Nikolaus Lenau
(1802-1850)

Lenau (a pseudonym for Nikolaus Niembsch von Strehlenau) was born in Hungary of German parents. Lenau is the very personification of Romantic longing. Like Hölderlin, he sought idyllic inner harmony in a world which seemed out of joint, and his lonely and tragic life also ended in insanity, which beclouded his mind during the last seven years. A born wanderer, he moved ceaselessly about Hungary and South Germany and in the year 1833 his quest for peace and happiness took him as far as the middle-west of the United States, a journey that ended in bitter disillusionment. A hopeless passion in his youth convinced him that above "every joy there hovers a threatening vulture."

Lenau's poems reflect his melancholy attitude to life and his restless strivings. Like no other poet he gives a most poignant expression to the *Weltschmerz* that obsessed him, that melancholy yet not totally unpleasurable despair of the world made fashionable by Byron. For comfort he flies to nature: but it mirrors only his own grief and woes. His compelling imagery, which evokes forsaken landscapes and an atmosphere of unrelieved misery compounded by the elegiac music of his lyrics, imparts to his *Weltschmerz* the ring of a deeply felt truth. His poems testify that pessimism and despair were inherent in his nature, that life is but an unending confirmation of his sincere conviction that joys lead but to suffering and that all hope is futile.

Lenau's dramatic treatment of *Faust* and *Don Juan* — the two archetypes of mankind's restless striving and longing for the ultimate — served as inspiration for Liszt's and Richard Strauss' symphonic works.

KOMMEN UND SCHEIDEN

So oft sie kam, erschien mir die Gestalt
So lieblich, wie das erste Grün im Wald.

Und was sie sprach, drang mir zum Herzen ein
Süss, wie des Frühlings erstes Lied im Hain.

Und als Lebwohl sie winkte mit der Hand,
War's, ob der letzte Jugendtraum mir schwand.

From the SCHILFLIEDER

Auf geheimem Waldespfade
Schleich' ich gern im Abendschein
An das öde Schilfgestade,
Mädchen, und gedenke dein!

Wenn sich dann der Busch verdüstert,
Rauscht das Rohr geheimnisvoll,
Und es klaget und es flüstert,
Dass ich weinen, weinen soll.

Und ich mein', ich höre wehen
Leise deiner Stimme Klang,
Und im Weiher untergehen
Deinen lieblichen Gesang.

ARRIVAL AND SEPARATION

Whenever she approached, her form to me appeared
As lovely as the first green in the woods.

And what she said, pierced my heart
Sʋeet as the spring's first song in the glade.

And when with her hand she waved farewell,
It was as if youth's final dream went from me.

From the SONGS OF THE REED

On secret woodland paths
I like to steal in evening's glow
To the desolate bulrush shore,
Maiden, and think of you.

When the bushes then grow darker,
Mysteriously rustles then the reed,
And it wails and whispers
That I should weep out, weep out.

And I seem to hear the sound
Of your voice gently floating
And your lovely song
Sinking in the pond.

Annette von Droste-Hülshoff
(1797-1848)

Annette von Droste-Hülshoff, Germany's greatest woman poet, strikes a persistently elegiac note reminiscent of Lenau. But unlike the latter's stark pessimism, hers is softened by a gentle note of pious resignation kindled and sustained by her Catholicism. Her life was one of renunciation, forced upon her partly by an unattractive appearance, by the life-long frailty of her body, and by a deep, hopeless love for a man much younger in years, the author Levin Schücking. From this unrequited love, sublimated into maternal affection, sprang most of her lyrics: her lyric powers were quickened by an uncanny and undoubtedly often painful awareness of her senses, an awareness which transformed the minutest realistic details of nature into the beauty of her verbal imagery. Her poems make us hear the caterpillar gnawing on a leaf, see a fish's shadow cast on the bottom of a lake, and feel her own heart pulsating as she lies daydreaming on the heath, gauging nature's sensitivity by her own. Because the backdrop of her lyrics are the moorlands of her Westphalian home in North Germany her poems are often called *Heimatdichtung* (regional poetry). Yet Droste-Hülshoff's deep psychological insight and unfeigned spiritual and emotional power give the local atmosphere she evokes a universality which transcends the surroundings she describes.

DER WEIHER

Er liegt so still im Morgenlicht,
So friedlich, wie ein fromm Gewissen;
Wenn Weste seinen Spiegel küssen,
Des Ufers Blume fühlt es nicht;
Libellen zittern über ihn,
Blaugoldne Stäbchen und Karmin,
Und auf des Sonnenbildes Glanz
Die Wasserspinne führt den Tanz;
Schwertlilienkranz am Ufer steht
Und horcht des Schilfes Schlummerliede;
Ein lindes Säuseln kommt und geht,
Als flüstre's: Friede! Friede! Friede!—

THE POND

It lies so quietly in the light of dawn,
As peaceful as a pious conscience;
When western winds its surface kiss
The lakeshore's flower does not feel it;
Dragonflies quiver above it,
Little rods of blue-gold and carmine,
And on the sun-reflection's gleam
The water spider does his dance;
At the shore wreaths of iris stand
And harken to the bulrush's lullaby;
A gentle rustling comes and goes
As though it whispered: Peace! Peace! Peace!—

Eduard Mörike
(1804-1875)

After a stormy youth which included a strange romance with a girl at once mystic and sensual, the Peregrina of his early poems, Mörike led a comparatively placid life as pastor of Swabian country parishes. His late marriage, however, was not tranquil and ended in separation. Mörike's latent talent as a painter is revealed in his poetry by an "innate urge to express graphically even the most abstract thoughts," to quote his contemporary, Theodor Storm. Thus in the first two stanzas of *Das verlassene Mägdlein*, he creates a vivid and well-observed picture. Beyond this, Mörike's poems (again the present one is a good example) are distinguished by the rare combination of realistic pictures, flowing rhythm, and musical sonority. The last two qualities have been appreciated by countless composers. Less than fifteen years after the poet's death, some fifty-odd song treatments of *Das verlassene Mägdlein* were produced. The best of these is Hugo Wolf's composition, which beautifully captures the melancholy, even tragic mood of the poem; a mood which pervades so many of Mörike's other poems.

DAS VERLASSENE MÄGDLEIN

Früh, wann*die Hähne krähn,
Eh' die Sternlein verschwinden,
Muss ich am Herde stehn,
Muss Feuer zünden.

Schön ist der Flammen Schein,
Es springen die Funken;
Ich schaue so drein,
In Leid versunken.

Plötzlich, da kommt es mir,
Treuloser Knabe,
Dass ich die Nacht von dir
Geträumet habe.

Träne auf Träne dann
Stürzet hernieder;
So kommt der Tag heran —
O ging' er wieder!

*In the recording this word was
inadvertently read as *wenn.*

THE JILTED GIRL

Early, when the roosters crow,
Before the little stars disappear,
I must stand by the hearth,
Must kindle the fire.

Beautiful is the flames' glow;
The sparks dance;
I gaze upon it,
Engulfed in sorrow.

Suddenly it occurs to me,
Faithless boy,
That I, last night,
Have dreamt of you.

Then tear upon tear
Rushes downward;
Thus day begins —
Oh, would it leave again.

Ludwig Uhland

(1787-1862)

A Swabian by birth like Hölderlin, Uhland was a poet, a scholar, and a liberal politician. After serving three years as professor of German literature at the University of Tübingen he was forced to resign because he was refused a leave of absence upon his election to the Diet of Swabia. After the revolution of 1848 he became a delegate to the Frankfurt Parliament. In a speech against the hereditary empire he demanded that Germany's rulers must be "anointed with the oil of democracy."

Many consider Uhland to be Germany's best writer of ballads next to Schiller. Like the latter, he often used the ballad form to champion an ethical ideal or to register a social protest. For the most part, however, Uhland tells the ballads for their own sake, imparting to them the simplicity of a folk song. Undoubtedly this simple folk-like quality accounts for the fact that many of his ballads, such as *Der Wirtin Töchterlein* and *Der gute Kamerad,* have been accepted as folk songs by the German people.

Apart from writing ballads with a folk-like quality, Uhland also collected and edited German folk songs; he was in fact the editor of the first scholarly edition of German folk songs to be published. Thus, he continued the tradition begun at the turn of the century by the Brothers Grimm, by Arnim and Brentano, collectors of *Des Knaben Wunderhorn (The Boy's Cornucopia* [of folk songs]), and other authors of the Romantic movement who sought to revive interest in Germany's cultural folk-heritage.

DER WIRTIN TÖCHTERLEIN

Es zogen drei Bursche wohl über den Rhein,
Bei einer Frau Wirtin, da kehrten sie ein:

"Frau Wirtin, hat Sie gut Bier und Wein?
Wo hat Sie Ihr schönes Töchterlein?"

Und als sie traten zur Kammer hinein,
Da lag sie in einem schwarzen Schrein.

Der erste, der schlug den Schleier zurück
Und schaute sie an mit traurigem Blick:

"Ach! lebtest du noch, du schöne Maid!
Ich würde dich lieben von dieser Zeit."

Der zweite deckte den Schleier zu
Und kehrte sich ab und weinte dazu:

"Ach! dass du liegst auf der Totenbahr'!
Ich hab' dich geliebet so manches Jahr."

Der dritte hub ihn wieder sogleich
Und küsste sie an den Mund so bleich:

"Dich liebt' ich immer, dich lieb' ich noch heut'
Und werde dich lieben in Ewigkeit."

THE INNKEEPER'S YOUNG DAUGHTER

Three fellows once crossed the Rhine;
They stopped at a lady-innkeeper's inn.

"Mrs. Innkeeper, do you have good beer and wine?
Where are you keeping your beautiful young daughter?"

And when they stepped into the room,
She was lying in a black coffin.

The first fellow drew back the veil
And looked at her with saddened glance.

"Oh, if you still lived, you beautiful girl,
I would love you henceforth."

The second lowered the veil again
And turned away and weepingly said:

"Oh, that you are lying upon the bier!
I have loved you for many a year."

The third at once lifted it up again
And kissed her upon her mouth so pale:

"I loved you always, I still love you today
And I shall love you through eternity."

Heinrich Heine
(1797-1856)

Next to Goethe, Heine has become Germany's best known poet abroad. Carried on the wings of Schumann's songs, poems like *Du bist wie eine Blume* and *Die zwei Grenadiere* have found homes in all parts of the world. Heine has rightfully been called the last poet of the Romantic Age, for in poems like *Im wunderschönen Monat Mai* the sentiments of that epoch once more find masterful expression: man and nature awaken in Maytime. This sentiment is expressed in the tones of the folk song which Heine and the Romantics tried to strike in their own works.

But Heine transcended the Romantic Age. In the words of his contemporary Eichendorff, "the times had become bored with the hollow games of the Romantics . . . and Heine broke the magic spell." All the poems which break the spell of the sentimental poetry employ an identical technique. In the first part of these poems he seemingly continues in the Romantic tradition; then he destroys this effect by "the cold shower" of the last part. Thus *Ich wollte,meine Lieder* seems to be a conventional love poem until Heine's irony disenchants the reader. He often does so by contrasting the lofty poetic words in the first part with the very prosaic terms in the second (for example, "peas," "peasoup," "cook"). Finally, some of his poems are completely dominated by political or social satire, or they become the receptacle for his devastating wit, which is often tinged with erotic allusions. Both wit and sensuality are present in his humorous poem *Mit dummen Mädchen.*

"MIT DUMMEN MÄDCHEN"

Mit dummen Mädchen, hab' ich gedacht,
Nichts ist mit dummen anzufangen;
Doch als ich mich an die klugen gemacht,
Da ist es mir noch schlimmer ergangen.

Die klugen waren mir viel zu klug,
Ihr Fragen machte mich ungeduldig,
Und wenn ich selber das Wichtigste frug,
Da blieben sie lachend die Antwort schuldig.

"IM WUNDERSCHÖNEN MONAT MAI"

Im wunderschönen Monat Mai,
Als alle Knospen sprangen,
Da ist in meinem Herzen
Die Liebe aufgegangen.

Im wunderschönen Monat Mai,
Als alle Vögel sangen,
Da hab' ich ihr gestanden
Mein Sehnen und Verlangen.

"WITH WITLESS GIRLS"

With witless girls, I have thought,
Nothing can be done with witless ones;
But when I approached the clever ones,
I fared even worse.

The clever ones were much too clever for me,
Their questions made me impatient,
And when I myself asked the most important thing,
They laughingly avoided an answer.

"IN THE WONDROUSLY BEAUTIFUL MONTH OF MAY"

In the wondrously beautiful month of May
When all the buds sprang open,
Then in my heart
Love sprouted.

In the wondrously beautiful month of May
When all the birds were singing,
Then I confessed to her
My longing and desire.

"ICH WOLLTE, MEINE LIEDER"

Ich wollte, meine Lieder
Das wären Blümelein:
Ich schickte sie zu riechen
Der Herzallerliebsten mein.

Ich wollte, meine Lieder
Das wären Küsse fein:
Ich schickt' sie heimlich alle
Nach Liebchens Wängelein.

Ich wollte, meine Lieder
Das wären Erbsen klein:
Ich kocht' eine Erbsensuppe,
Die sollte köstlich sein.

"I WISH THAT ALL MY SONGS"

I wish that all my songs
Were little flowers:
I would send them to be smelled
By the darling of my heart.

I wish that all my songs
Were delicate kisses:
I secretly would send them all
To my sweetheart's little cheek.

I wish that all my songs
Were little peas:
I would cook a peasoup
Which would really be delicious.

August Graf von Platen
(1796-1835)

"In the future I shall use only the most stringent discipline in my work" and "Only a person who has become an absolute master of form and language may call himself an artist in every sense of the word." Count von Platen sought to live up to these self-set canons by iron self-discipline and absolute devotion to his art. His *Wille zur Form* or will toward aesthetic form was in part a reaction to the prevailing Romantic Movement which he felt sacrificed, all too often, form to emotional impact. As a result Platen's poems may at times lack depth of feeling but they reach unequaled perfection in form: no extra syllable mars the rhythm and no impure rhyme offends the ear.

The ballad *Das Grab im Busento* offers a glimpse into the methodology of a poet who strove for perfection and to whom intricate verse forms and complex rhyme schemes were a challenge rather than a deterrent. Platen was inspired to compose the ballad after reading Gibbon's description in *The Decline and Fall of the Roman Empire* of the grandiose burial of the Visigoth King Alaric (A.D. 410), whose valor the Goths celebrated not only with "mournful applause" but by forcing thousands of their Roman captives to divert the course of the river Busentinus in order to provide in the vacant bed a place for the royal sepulchre "adorned with the splendid spoils and trophies of Rome." Then, as Gibbon relates, "the waters were restored to their natural channel; and the secret spot was forever concealed by the inhuman massacre of the prisoners." This episode with its brutal ending would seem to offer scant material for a heroic ballad. But Platen shaped his material to his poetic purpose. He deleted the massacre of the prisoners and the "mournful applause" becomes a chant of glory. He invented details — such as the king being buried in his armor and high on horseback — which turn Gibbon's prosaic account into a poetic vision through graphic and statuesque imagery. But even this was only the first step: once the first version was written, Platen recast the poem several times; he doubled the length of the lines over the original and tested every word for its aptness and effect. As a result, the long lines of the final version — with their eight accented syllables in perfect trochaic measure—suggest perfectly the mournful yet forceful march of the army's funeral procession while the careful choice of sonorous and majestic words infuses a heroic spirit into every line.

DAS GRAB IM BUSENTO

Nächtlich am Busento lispeln bei Cosenza dumpfe
  Lieder,
Aus den Wassern schallt es Antwort, und in Wirbeln klingt
  es wider.

Und den Fluss hinauf, hinunter ziehn die
  Schatten tapfrer Goten,
Die den Alarich beweinen, ihres Volkes besten
  Toten.

Allzufrüh und fern der Heimat mussten hier sie
  ihn begraben,
Während noch die Jugendlocken seine Schultern blond
  umgaben.

Und am Ufer des Busento reihten sie sich um die
  Wette,
Um die Strömung abzuleiten, gruben sie ein frisches Bette.

In der wogenleeren Höhlung wühlten sie empor
  die Erde,
Senkten tief hinein den Leichnam, mit der Rüstung, auf
  dem Pferde.

Deckten dann mit Erde wieder ihn und seine stolze
  Habe,
Dass die hohen Stromgewächse wüchsen aus
  dem Heldengrabe.

Abgelenkt zum zweiten Male, ward der Fluss
  herbeigezogen:
Mächtig in ihr altes Bette schäumten die
  Busentowogen.

THE GRAVE IN THE BUSENTO

At the shores of the Busento muffled songs are
   whispered nightly near Cosenza;
From the waters rings forth answer and in the whirlpools
   sounds an echo!

And stream-upward and stream-downward move
   the shades of valiant Goths,
Who weep for Alaric, the best departed of their
   people.

All too early, far from home, they were forced
   to entomb him here,
While his curls, blond and youthful, still around
   his shoulders fell.

And on the shores of the Busento they formed ranks,
   each vied with each,
To divert the current a new river-bed they dug.

In the hollow, void of waves, they were turning up the
   ground,
Into it they lowered deeply the dead body,
   in its armor and on horseback.

Then they covered him again, him with his proud
   possessions,
That the tall river plants might sprout from the hero's
   grave.

For the second time diverted, the river was drawn
   near:
Mighty, the Busento waves foamed into their old
   bed.

Und es sang ein Chor von Männern: "Schlaf in deinen
   Heldenehren!
Keines Römers schnöde Habsucht soll dir je dein
   Grab versehren!"

Sangen's, und die Lobgesänge tönten fort im
   Gotenheere;
Wälze sie, Busentowelle, wälze sie von Meer
   zu Meere!

And a choir of men was singing: "Sleep upon your
hero's honor!
Never shall your grave be despoiled by the vile greed of
a Roman!"

So they sang and the songs of praise rang forth
in the Gothic ranks;
Roll them onward, Busento waves, roll them on from
sea to sea!

Friedrich Rückert
(1788-1866)

Like many of the writers and poets of the Romantic Period, Rückert was both a scholar and a poet. He taught Oriental languages, first at the University of Erlangen, later in Berlin. His interpretation of Oriental culture and literature and his translations from Arabic and Sanskrit won him wide acclaim. Goethe — who late in life had also been inspired by Oriental poetry, as exemplified in his *West-Östlicher Divan*— hailed Rückert as a worthy fellow-worker in the common task of stimulating their countrymen's interest in world literature. As a poet Rückert, however, owes his reputation less to his virtuosity in imitating the intricate patterns of Oriental stanzas, such as the Persian gazel, than to his patriotic lyrics during the War of Liberation from Napoleon, poems such as the *Geharnischte Sonette* (Sonnets in Armor) and simpler folk lyrics, such as *Liebesfrühling* (Spring of Love) from which this selection is taken. The unaffected emotion and quiet serenity of this poem has been magically captured by Franz Schubert's composition, *Du bist die Ruh'*. Many other of Rückert's poems live on by virtue of the musical settings by Brahms, while his cycle of songs *Kindertotenlieder* (Songs on the Death of Children), written after the death of his two children, will survive in Gustav Mahler's musical rendition.

KEHR' EIN BEI MIR!

Du bist die Ruh',
Der Friede mild,
Die Sehnsucht du
Und was sie stillt.

Ich weihe dir
Voll Lust und Schmerz
Zur Wohnung hier
Mein Aug' und Herz.

Kehr' ein bei mir,
Und schliesse du
Still hinter dir
Die Pforten zu.

Treib' andern Schmerz
Aus dieser Brust!
Voll sei dies Herz
Von deiner Lust.

Dies Augenzelt
Von deinem Glanz
Allein erhellt,
O füll' es ganz.

ALIGHT WITH ME

You are repose,
Tranquility mild,
You are longing
And what fulfills it.

To you I dedicate
Full of joy and sorrow
As dwelling place
My eyes and heart.

Alight with me
And then lock
Quietly behind you
The portals.

Drive other sorrow
From this breast,
Let this heart be filled
By your delights.

This canopy of my eyes
From your lustre
Alone lights up.
Oh, fill it completely.

Viktor von Scheffel

(1826-1886)

When Victor von Scheffel was a university student, he found the life of the *Burschenschaften* (German fraternities), with their zest for outings and lengthy drinking bouts, much more to his liking than the lectures at the university. Out of this rollicking period in his life came a collection of poems, significantly bearing the old Latin motto *Gaudeamus* (Let's be merry), which are nearly as popular among students today as when Scheffel first wrote them about a hundred years ago. Sung to traditional tunes or to the melodies by various German composers, Scheffel's early poetry has become part of the standard repertory of university song-fests. It is easy to understand why, for the poet extols the virtues of a free student life and satirizes professors and the various arts and sciences, from literature to geology. In the poem *Altassyrisch* cultural history serves as the butt of his joke. Here Scheffel uses one of his favorite devices; he carelessly mixes allusions to the distant past (the cuneiform characters) and allusions to biblical history (the story of Jonah and the whale) with unmistakable references to modern times (the clock which strikes the hour). The result is a very funny potpourri of anachronisms—and also tells a truth which students and other carousers have experienced throughout the ages.

ALTASSYRISCH

Im Schwarzen Walfisch zu Askalon
Da trank ein Mann drei Tag',
Bis dass er steif wie ein Besenstiel
Am Marmortische lag.

Im Schwarzen Walfisch zu Askalon
Da sprach der Wirt: "Halt an!
Der trinkt von meinem Dattelsaft
Mehr als er zahlen kann."

Im Schwarzen Walfisch zu Askalon
Da bracht' der Kellner Schar
In Keilschrift auf sechs Ziegelstein
Dem Gast die Rechnung dar.

Im Schwarzen Walfisch zu Askalon
Da sprach der Gast: "O weh!
Mein bares Geld ging alles drauf
Im Lamm zu Niniveh!"

Im Schwarzen Walfisch zu Askalon
Da schlug die Uhr halb vier,
Da warf der Hausknecht aus Nubierland
Den Fremden vor die Tür.

Im Schwarzen Walfisch zu Askalon
Wird kein Prophet geehrt,
Und wer vergnügt dort leben will,
Zahlt bar, was er verzehrt.

OLD ASSYRIAN

At the Black Whale in Ascalon
A man drank for three days
Until, as stiff as a broomstick,
He lay on the marble table.

At the Black Whale in Ascalon
The innkeeper said: "Enough!"
He's drinking of my date juice
More than he can ever pay."

At the Black Whale in Ascalon
A drove of waiters brought —
On six tiles in cuneiform—
The bill up to the guest.

At the Black Whale in Ascalon
The guest he said: "Alas!
All my cash went by the boards
At the Lamb in Niniveh!"

At the Black Whale in Ascalon
The clock was striking four,
Then the porter from Nubia threw
The stranger out the door.

At the Black Whale in Ascalon
No prophet is respected,
And who wants to live in pleasure there,
Pays cash for what he consumes.

Detlev von Liliencron
(1844-1909)

Liliencron turned poet at the age of forty, when he resigned from the German army because of severe injuries sustained in battle. The two poems below reflect, in a way, the career of this officer-turned-poet. As in many of his poems, he is able to convey a fleeting series of impressions, gathered during his military service. In *Die Musik kommt* he uses an impressionistically colorful sequence of pictures and a series of masterful onomatopoetic descriptions to make us both see and hear the military procession. We first hear the music approaching from the distance — then we hear windows and lanterns vibrate from the crescendo of the instruments and the pounding steps as the regiment passes right in front of us — and finally we listen to the sounds dying away in the distance. The entire village — and with it Liliencron — thrills with delight at the sight of the soldiers on parade. But Liliencron who had fought in the Austro-Prussian war of 1866 and the Franco-Prussian war of 1870-1871 was equally aware of the pall of suffering and death cast over a dashing parade of soldiers. *Wer weiss wo* is almost an anti-war poem. Suddenly the cheerful sounds of the peace-time parade are transmuted into sounds which "did not sound gay": the grief of a father at the news of his youngster's death.

DIE MUSIK KOMMT

Klingling, bumbum und tschingdada,
Zieht im Triumph der Perserschah?
Und um die Ecke brausend bricht's
Wie Tubaton des Weltgerichts,
    Voran der Schellenträger.

Brumbrum, das grosse Bombardon,
Der Beckenschlag, das Helikon,
Die Pikkolo, der Zinkenist,
Die Türkentrommel, der Flötist,
    Und dann der Herre Hauptmann.

Der Hauptmann naht mit stolzem Sinn,
Die Schuppenketten unterm Kinn,
Die Schärpe schnürt den schlanken Leib,
Beim Zeus! Das ist kein Zeitvertreib;
    Und dann die Herren Leutnants.

Zwei Leutnants, rosenrot und braun,
Die Fahne schützen sie als Zaun;
Die Fahne kommt, den Hut nimm ab,
Der bleiben treu wir bis ans Grab!
    Und dann die Grenadiere.

Die Grenadier im strammen Tritt,
In Schritt und Tritt und Tritt und Schritt,
Das stampft und dröhnt und klappt und flirrt,
Laternenglas und Fenster klirrt,
    Und dann die kleinen Mädchen.

THE MUSIC'S COMING

Ding-dong, bang-bang, tshingdada,
Is it a procession triumphant of the Persian shah?
And around the corner it breaks forth with a roar
Like the tuba's tone of the judgment day,
    Out in front the bearer of the crescent.

Bum-bum, the giant bombardon,
The cymbals and the helicon,
The piccolo, the bugle player,
The Turkish drum and the flutist,
    And then the Mr. Captain.

The captain's approaching with feelings proud,
The chinstraps underneath his chin,
The sash straps 'round his slender waist.
By Jove, that is no idle pastime,
    And then come the lieutenants.

Two lieutenants, rosy-red and brown,
The flag they're guarding as a living fence;
The flag's approaching, raise your hat,
We'll stay faithful to it till our death!
    And then the grenadiers.

The grenadiers in rigid step,
In step and stride, and stride and step,
That stamps, and thuds, and rattles, and flits,
The glass of lanterns, windows jingle,
    And then the little girls.

Die Mädchen alle, Kopf an Kopf,
Das Auge blau und blond der Zopf,
Aus Tür und Tor und Hof und Haus
Schaut Mine, Trine, Stine aus,
Vorbei ist die Musike.

Klingkling, tschingtsching und Paukenkrach,
Noch aus der Ferne tönt es schwach,
Ganz leise bumbumbumbum tsching;
Zog da ein bunter Schmetterling,
Tschingtsching, bum, um die Ecke?

The little girls all, head to head,
Their eyes of blue and blond their pigtails,
From door and gate and yard and house
Minnie, Kitty, Chris look out,
    Past now is the music.

Ding-dong, tshing-tshing, and kettle drums' roar,
Still weakly from the distance sounds
So softly, bumbumbumbum, tshing,
Did just now a colored butterfly turn,
    Tshing-tshing bum, 'round the corner?

WER WEISS WO
Schlacht bei Kolin, 18. Juni 1757

Auf Blut und Leichen, Schutt und Qualm,
Auf rosszerstampften Sommerhalm
Die Sonne schien.
Es sank die Nacht. Die Schlacht ist aus,
Und mancher kehrte nicht nach Haus
Einst von Kolin.

Ein Junker auch, ein Knabe noch,
Der heut das erste Pulver roch,
Er musste dahin.
Wie hoch er auch die Fahne schwang,
Der Tod in seinen Arm ihn zwang,
Er musste dahin.

Ihm nahe lag ein frommes Buch,
Das stets der Junker bei sich trug,
Am Degenknauf.
Ein Grenadier von Bevern fand
Den kleinen erdbeschmutzten Band
Und hob ihn auf.

Und brachte heim mit schnellem Fuss
Dem Vater diesen letzten Gruss,
der klang nicht froh.
Dann schrieb hinein die Zitterhand:
"Kolin. Mein Sohn verscharrt im Sand.
Wer weiss wo."

Und der gesungen dieses Lied,
Und der es liest, im Leben zieht
Noch frisch und froh.
Doch einst bin ich, und bist auch du,
Verscharrt im Sand zur ewigen Ruh,
Wer weiss wo.

WHO KNOWS WHERE
Battle of Kolin, June 18, 1757

Upon blood and corpses, rubble, smoke,
Upon horse-betrampled summer stalks
The sun shone down.
Nightfall descended. The battle's done,
And many did not homeward come
Then from Kolin.

A cadet too, still just a boy,
Who his first gunsmoke smelled today,
He had to go.
No matter how high he swung the flag,
Into his arms Death forced him,
He had to go.

A pious book lay close to him,
Which the cadet always bore with him
On his sword's handle.
A grenadier from Bevern found
The small and earth-bespattered volume
And picked it up.

And carried home with quickened step
This final greeting to the father,
It did not sound gay.
Then wrote the trembling hand therein:
"Kolin. My son buried in the sand.
Who knows where."

And he who has intoned this song,
And he who reads it, walks in life
Still brisk and happy.
But someday I, and also you, will be
Interred in sand to rest eternal
Who knows where.

Conrad Ferdinand Meyer

(1825-1898)

Conrad Ferdinand Meyer, a Swiss novelist and poet, produced his relatively small collection of creative works only by dint of the greatest effort. Rarely satisfied with the first version of his poems, he constantly revised and refined them. As a result of his methods, he created a work in his poem *Der römische Brunnen* which is well-nigh perfect in form. Practically every syllable has its specific function in the poem's architecture. Thus the three-tier fountain has its parallel in three verse pairs (lines 1 to 6); the rising jet of water is reproduced in the first line by a spondee, that is by two accented "rising" syllables, which Meyer produces by boldly disregarding the rules of conventional German grammar (which would force the prefix *auf* to the end of the clause). Finally, as a comparison with an earlier version indicates, Meyer deliberately shortened the last line, in order to give added emphasis to the two accented words *strömt* and *ruht,* which are meant to convey the main thought of the poem. Meyer, by the form and content of his poem — and especially by these two words of the last line — tells us that the seeming antitheses in life — repose and motion, giving and taking, freedom and restraint, rise and fall — can be brought into harmony. By the form and imagery of his poem he demonstrates the feasibility of his convictions.

DER RÖMISCHE BRUNNEN

Aufsteigt der Strahl und fallend giesst
Er voll der Marmorschale Rund,
Die, sich verschleiernd, überfliesst
In einer zweiten Schale Grund;
Die zweite gibt, sie wird zu reich,
Der dritten wallend ihre Flut,
Und jede nimmt und gibt zugleich
Und strömt und ruht.

THE ROMAN FOUNTAIN

The jet ascends, and, falling, fills
Replete the marble basin's sphere,
Which — enveiling itself — overflows
Into the bottom of a second bowl;
The second passes, grown too full,
Its flood, in waves, on to the third,
And each receives and gives, at the same time,
And flows and rests.

Friedrich Nietzsche
(1844-1900)

Nietzsche was not only a powerful philosopher but also an excellent lyric poet, a master stylist in prose and verse. Indeed, some of his philosophic treatises, such as *Thus Spake Zarathustra*, read more like poetry than prose.

The poem *Vereinsamt* has been described as "perhaps the loneliest poem ever written." It is a deeply touching expression of the inner turmoil and tragic life of a man whose philosophic message was the vigorous and exuberant affirmation of life under all conditions; a man who regarded tragedy as the source of new life and power. After a brillant start in an academic career — on the basis of his prior achievements he was appointed professor of classical philology at the University of Basel at the age of twenty-three—Nietzsche soon resigned his post because of poor health. For the next ten years he lived a lonely wanderer's life, mostly in the Swiss Alps and Italy, in continual search of a favorable climate, tormented by excruciating headaches, stomach pains and insomnia which he could overcome only with ever increasing doses of barbiturates. Then, in 1889, he suffered a complete mental breakdown from which he did not recover in the eleven years left to him.

VEREINSAMT

Die Krähen schrein
Und ziehen schwirren Flugs zur Stadt:
Bald wird es schnein —
Wohl dem, der jetzt noch eine[*] Heimat hat!

Nun stehst du starr,
Schaust rückwärts, ach! wie lange schon!
Was bist du, Narr,
Vor Winters in die Welt entflohn?

Die Welt — ein Tor
Zu tausend Wüsten stumm und kalt!
Wer das verlor,
Was du verlorst, macht nirgends halt.

Nun stehst du bleich,
Zur Winterwanderschaft verflucht,
Dem Rauche gleich,
Der stets nach kältern Himmeln sucht.

Flieg, Vogel, schnarr'
Dein Lied im Wüstenvogelton! —
Versteck', du Narr,
Dein blutend Herz in Eis und Hohn!

Die Krähen schrein
Und ziehen schwirren Flugs zur Stadt:
Bald wird es schnein,
Weh dem, der keine **Heimat hat**!

*In the recording this word was inadver-
tently omitted.

ISOLATED

The crows caw
And are city-bound in whirring flight:
Soon it will snow —
Lucky he who now still has a home!

Here you stand petrified,
Gazing backward, alas! for oh, how long!
Why have you, fool,
At winter's gate fled forth into the world?

The world — a gate
To a thousand wastelands, mute and cold!
Whoever lost
What you have lost, finds nowhere rest.

Now you stand pale,
Condemned to wintry wandering,
Like smoke,
Which always seeks the colder climes.

Fly, bird, burr
Your song in strains of wasteland-birds! —
Hide, you fool,
Your bleeding heart in ice and scorn!

The crows caw
And are city-bound in whirring flight:
Soon it will snow —
Woe to him who has no home!

Christian Morgenstern
(1871-1914)

Morgenstern's verses of almost untranslatable "superior nonsense" rise considerably above the usual level of humorous lyrics because his absurdities often hide a serious indictment of our bourgeois mores and taboos. His whimsical satire is perhaps best illustrated by the following "mute" poem:

Songs of Fishes Under Water

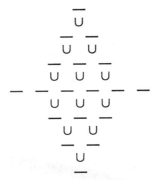

Morgenstern's special gift lies in revealing the grotesque irrationality of language (if there is an *Elefant* why should there not also be a *Zwölfant?* he asks, tongue-in-cheek) and in using words and sounds with an unexpected, freakish originality, such as in *Die Behörde (The Government Office)* in which Morgenstern derides German gobbledygook. In *Der Werwolf* he pokes fun at the declension of the German interrogative *wer* (who) by inventing a *Weswolf* "whosewolf"), a *Wemwolf* ("to-whom-wolf"), etc. Morgenstern would surely have agreed with Mark Twain — and countless students of German — that he would "rather decline a drink than decline a German noun."

DER WERWOLF

Ein Werwolf eines Nachts entwich
von Weib und Kind und sich begab
an eines Dorfschullehrers Grab
und bat ihn: Bitte, beuge mich!

Der Dorfschulmeister stieg hinauf
auf seines Blechschilds Messingknauf
und sprach zum Wolf, der seine Pfoten
geduldig kreuzte vor dem Toten:

"Der Werwolf" — sprach der gute Mann,
"des Weswolfs, Genitiv sodann,
dem Wemwolf, Dativ, wie man's nennt,
den Wenwolf, — damit hat's ein End."

Dem Werwolf schmeichelten die Fälle,
er rollte seine Augenbälle.
"Indessen, bat er, füge doch
zur Einzahl auch die Mehrzahl noch!"

Der Dorfschulmeister aber musste
gestehn, dass er von ihr nichts wusste.
Zwar Wölfe gab's in grosser Schar,
doch "Wer" gab's nur im Singular.

Der Wolf erhob sich tränenblind —
er hatte ja doch Weib und Kind!!
Doch da er kein Gelehrter eben,
so schied er dankbar und ergeben.

THE WEREWOLF

A werewolf one night got away
from his wife and child and ventured to
the grave of a village schoolteacher
and asked him: Please, decline me!

The village schoolmaster ascended
upon the brass knob of his tin gravemarker
and said to the wolf, who crossed his paws
patiently before the dead man:

"Der Werwolf" — said the good man,
"des Weswolfs, genitive is next,
dem Wemwolf, dative, as it's called,
den Wenwolf, — and with that it's finished."

The werewolf was flattered by the cases,
he rolled his eyeballs.
"However," he begged, "please add
to the singular also the plural!"

The village schoolmaster, however, had to
confess that he knew nothing of the plural.
Wolves, to be sure, existed in large numbers,
but "Who" occurs only in the singular.

The wolf arose, blinded by tears —
he had, recall, both wife and child!
But since he was not exactly a scholar,
he departed, grateful and resigned.

Richard Dehmel
(1863-1920)

Richard Dehmel's powerful poems strike many themes: he shows the struggle between the generations, extols the healthy life in the country as opposed to the degeneration of life in the cities, advocates a dionysiac life, and all but sanctifies sex as a "cosmic urge." But Dehmel is best known in Germany as a poet of social protest. Few poets appealed so directly to the German workers of his time, who affectionately called him "Vater Dehmel" and sang his *Erntelied* (Harvest Song) at innumerable workers' meetings. This wide-spread popularity prevailed despite the fact — or perhaps because of it — that Dehmel was not doctrinaire in his views. His sympathies went out to all forms of suffering and he writes movingly of an altruistic love for the whole of humanity: "Ich steh und prüfe die bestandne Fahrt: / nur Eine Inbrunst lässt sich treu ertragen: / zur ganzen Welt." (I stop and re-examine the past course of life: / only one passion can faithfully be borne: / that to the whole world.)

Although Dehmel came to reject Naturalism — his poems foreshadow both Symbolism and Expressionism — *Der Arbeitsmann* is symptomatic of the literature of Naturalism at the turn of the century. As so many poems of this literary movement, which often exposed the seamy side of human existence, *Der Arbeitsmann* focussed its attention on the social problems created by the rapid expansion of industrialism. Typical of the *Armeleutepoesie,* or "Poor people's poetry,". of the time, it expresses pity for the exploited, weary working man. Dehmel, the son of a forest-warden, was in love with the open spaces of his native Spreewald (north-eastern Germany) and envisioned a society in which the worker's most precious possession, time, is restored to him so that he can spend it in communing with nature.

Der Arbeitsmann was awarded first prize in a contest for the best poem of the "German working people," a contest organized in 1896 by the famous political-satiric weekly *Simplizissimus.*

DER ARBEITSMANN

Wir haben ein Bett, wir haben ein Kind,
mein Weib!
Wir haben auch Arbeit, und gar zu zweit,
und haben die Sonne und Regen und Wind,
und uns fehlt nur eine Kleinigkeit,
um so frei zu sein, wie die Vögel sind:
    Nur Zeit.

Wenn wir Sonntags durch die Felder gehn,
mein Kind,
und über den Ahren weit und breit
das blaue Schwalbenvolk blitzen sehn,
oh, dann fehlt uns nicht* das bisschen Kleid,
um so schön zu sein, wie die Vögel sind:
    Nur Zeit.

Nur Zeit! wir wittern Gewitterwind,
wir Volk.
Nur eine kleine Ewigkeit;
uns fehlt ja nichts, mein Weib, mein Kind,
als all das, was durch uns gedeiht,
um so kühn zu sein, wie die Vögel sind:
    Nur Zeit!

*In the recording this word was inadver-
tently read as *nur.*

THE WORKINGMAN

We have a bed, we have a child,
my wife!
We also have work, both of us too,
and we have the sun and the rain and the wind.
And we lack just a trifle
to be as free as the birds:
    Only time.

When we walk on Sundays over the fields,
my child,
and over the ears of grain far and wide
we see the blue swallows like lightning streak forth,
oh then we do not lack a bit of clothing
to be as beautiful as the birds are:
    Only time.

Only time! We sense a thunderous wind,
we people.
Only a short eternity;
we truly lack nothing, my wife, my child,
but all the things which prosper through us,
to be just as bold as the birds:
    Only time!

Hugo von Hofmannsthal

(1874-1929)

Hugo von Hofmannsthal is probably best known outside of his native Austria as the author of the morality play *Jedermann* (Everyman), which is performed every year at the Salzburg Festival, and as the librettist for Richard Strauss' operas *Der Rosenkavalier, Elektra, Die Frau ohne Schatten, Arabella,* and *Ariadne auf Naxos.* But among German-speaking people he is equally respected for his lyric gift which pervades his poems as well as his dramas and librettos. His talent sprang forth, almost full-grown, when Hofmannsthal was only seventeen years old. Even at that age his verses had the music, the sonorous sound, the restraint, and somber seriousness which characterizes the later poem *Die Beiden.* The form of the poem is a variation on the sonnet structure: the number of lines are those of the traditional sonnet; the rhyme scheme is not. The very choice of this form shows the discipline and economy which Hofmannsthal exercises as a poet. Not a single unnecessary word is said. The first stanza introduces us to the young girl; the chiselled beauty of her face stands before us by means of a single simile, which equates the roundness and regularity of her features with the same qualities of the goblet, while her grace is revealed by the lightness and sureness of her walk. The young man is presented in a similar manner; his hand is as steady in controlling a young horse as hers is in the performance of her feminine task of offering the goblet. In the last part of the poem, when these two young steady hands fail to meet because they tremble so, the poet has communicated a primary emotion not by telling us of the emotion in the abstract, but by embodying it in the hands of the two young lovers, "the twosome," as they are appropriately called in the title.

DIE BEIDEN

Sie trug den Becher in der Hand,
— Ihr Kinn und Mund glich seinem Rand —,
So leicht und sicher war ihr Gang,
Kein Tropfen aus dem Becher sprang.

So leicht und fest war seine Hand:
Er ritt auf einem jungen Pferde,
Und mit nachlässiger Gebärde
Erzwang er, dass es zitternd stand.

Jedoch wenn er aus ihrer Hand
Den leichten Becher nehmen sollte,
So war es beiden allzu schwer:
Denn beide bebten sie so sehr,
Dass keine Hand die andre fand
Und dunkler Wein am Boden rollte.

THE TWOSOME

She carried the goblet in her hand
— Her chin and mouth were like its rim —
So light and sure was her walk,
That not a drop sprang from the goblet.

So light and firm was his hand:
He rode upon a young horse,
And with a careless gesture
He forced it to halt, atremble.

When he, however, from her hand
The weightless goblet was to take,
It was too difficult for both:
For both were trembling so much,
That neither hand found the other
And dark wine rolled to the ground.

Stefan George

(1868-1933)

Stefan George brought about a reform in German poetry by reviving the canon of art for art's sake after the fashion of the French Parnassians and Symbolists. By means of his art journal, *Blätter für die Kunst,* and his own poems he became the poet-priest of a small circle of German aesthetes who worshipped absolute perfection of form as the supreme canon of poetry. According to George, the poet who is the judge and seer of his time, should speak for the chosen few only, and his device of spelling nouns with small letters and omitting punctuation marks was intended as a "barbed-wire fence against the unbidden ones." But George also set his stamp on the poetic language of Germany: he made it more stern and sparing and utilized sounds in extraordinary and richer combinations.

The poem included in this selection is a love poem. But the fact that the emotion of love is not described or analyzed but conveyed by impressions cast in flawless meter and delicately chiseled architecture also makes it George's confession of his artistic credo: the skillful blending of images and sounds, of thought and form.

"DU SCHLANK UND REIN WIE EINE FLAMME"

Du schlank und rein wie eine flamme
Du wie der morgen zart und licht
Du blühend reis vom edlen stamme
Du wie ein quell geheim und schlicht

Begleitest mich auf sonnigen matten
Umschauerst mich im abendrauch
Erleuchtest meinen weg im schatten
Du kühler wind du heisser hauch

Du bist mein wunsch und mein gedanke
Ich atme dich mit jeder luft
Ich schlürfe dich mit jedem tranke
Ich küsse dich mit jedem duft

Du blühend reis vom edlen stamme
Du wie ein quell geheim und schlicht
Du schlank und rein wie eine flamme
Du wie der morgen zart und licht

"YOU SLIM AND PURE JUST
LIKE A FLAME"

You slim and pure just like a flame
You just like morning bright and tender
You blossoming sprig on a proud stem
You like a spring concealed and plain

You accompany me on sunny mountain meadows
Surround me in the mist of eve
You light my pathway in the shadow
You cooling wind, you fiery breath

You are my wish and are my thought
I breathe you with each breath of air
I sip you with each drink
I kiss you with each fragrant odor

You blossoming sprig on a proud stem
You like a spring concealed and plain
You slim and pure just like a flame
You just like morning bright and tender

Rainer Maria Rilke

(1875-1926)

Like Stefan George, Rilke sought to create poems that were flawless works of art, impeccable in alliteration, assonance, rhyme, and rhythm. Rilke held that the act of poetic creation was not only the result of inspiration but of a hard-working craftsman grappling with his medium. In his *Dinggedichte* (thing-poems) Rilke imparted a startlingly new vision and refreshingly poetic vigor to the things outworn and obscured by every-day life and to "the poor words starving from commonplace usage." Thanks to his loving concern for animate and inanimate objects — a caged panther or a staircase — the German language itself became an even more refined and sensitive poetic instrument.

Spanische Tänzerin is taken from *Neue Gedichte (New Poems)*, a collection of lyrics written under the influence of Auguste Rodin and dedicated to him. Rilke had accepted the job as Rodin's secretary for the sake of studying the man whom he considered to be his mentor and model. Rilke's association with the French sculptor brought about a most significant turn in his poetic career, for he advanced from his earlier impressionistic aestheticism to a peculiarly objective and sculpturesque form.

By a masterful blending of visual and sound metaphors — note the hissing sibilants of the sharp scratch of a match and the spurt and sputter of the flame interrupted by the staccato bursts of *k* and *t*-sounds suggesting the castanets — Rilke apprehends and captures the very essence of the explosive *ambiente* of the flamenco dance. Note how the sharp, sculpture-like outlines of the dancer are transformed into tensely dynamic motion as the verses seem to writhe sinuously as the meaning of one line overflows into the next. Now they seem to twist and twirl, coil and recoil, snake-like, with the apposition of short and long words and tension-strained pauses signaling the unlocking of emotional floodgates. Suddenly the dancer crystallizes before us: a fiery fusion of art and artist, object and subject, sound and meaning. But the poem is more than that. It is also the art of the Flamenco as a manifestation of inherent erotic ardor and its embodiment in a temptress whose serpentine movements and naked arms ending in rattling castanets* seek to ensnare us by the treacherously-enticing call of Passion, surcharged, uninhibited, and Spanish.

* *klappern* (to rattle) and *Schlange* (snake) combine to suggest *Klapperschlange* (rattle-snake) .

SPANISCHE TÄNZERIN

Wie in der Hand ein Schwefelzündholz, weiss,
eh es zur Flamme kommt, nach allen Seiten
zuckende Zungen streckt — : beginnt im Kreis
naher Beschauer hastig, hell und heiss
ihr runder Tanz sich zuckend auszubreiten.

Und plötzlich ist er Flamme ganz und gar.

Mit ihrem Blick entzündet sie ihr Haar
und dreht auf einmal mit gewagter Kunst
ihr ganzes Kleid in diese Feuersbrunst,
aus welcher sich, wie Schlangen, die erschrecken,
die nackten Arme wach und klappernd strecken.

Und dann: als würde ihr das Feuer knapp,
nimmt sie es ganz zusamm und wirft es ab
sehr herrisch, mit hochmütiger Gebärde
und schaut: da liegt es rasend auf der Erde
und flammt noch immer und ergibt sich nicht —.
Doch sieghaft, sicher und mit einem süssen
grüssenden Lächeln hebt sie ihr Gesicht
und stampft es aus mit kleinen festen Füssen.

SPANISH DANCER

As in one's hand, a matchstick, white,
before it bursts to flame, to every side
extends its flashing tongues — : so begins in a circle
of close observers, hastily, bright and hot
her circular dance to spread out flashing.

And all at once it's flame entire.

Her hair she kindles with her glance
and suddenly with daring art she turns
her total dress into this conflagration,
from out of which, like serpents which are frightened,
her naked arms extend, awake and rattling.

And then: as if the fire grew too scant for her,
she gathers it completely, throws it off
very imperiously, with a haughty gesture
and looks: there it lies raging on the ground
as yet still flame and it does not surrender —.
But she, triumphant, self-assured, and with a sweet
Saluting smile lifts up her face
And stamps it out with feet both small and firm.

Hermann Hesse

(1877-1962)

Hermann Hesse, one of the triumvirate of German Nobel Prize winners*, excels in a type of poetry which Germans call *Gedankenlyrik* (philosophical poetry). Though influenced by the philosophers of the German Romantic Movement, by Nietzsche, Goethe, and various other European philosophers, Hesse's works also reflect his preoccupation with thoughts of China and India (where his parents had lived for many years and which he visited in 1911). In the poem *Ich liebe Frauen* these Oriental philosophies are clearly discernible. Man's soul, as well as all matter, living or dead, is part of an enduring universe. Man has no more importance in this total cosmos than any other object and he should therefore "call with loving name even animal and stone," to quote one of Hesse's poems. The poet indicates this equality of man and matter in *Ich liebe Frauen* by deliberately reversing the order in which he speaks of women and cities when he repeats his theme in stanzas three and four.

The poem also suggests that Man continues to live by a process of transmigration of the soul, a concept which Hesse likewise borrows from Hindu philosophy. If one believes in this type of continued existence, the boundaries of time and space disappear; the poet can fall in love with the women and cities of the past — and of the future. Hesse envisions a future in which his ideals find fulfilment; where the beauty of his visions finds its equal in reality. This thought, expressed in the climactic last line, is emphasized by the repetition of the word *Schönheit*, which forces the reader to come to a complete stop before reading the pregnant last part of the line.

* Gerhart Hauptmann and Thomas Mann are the other two Nobel Prize winners for literature.

"ICH LIEBE FRAUEN"

Ich liebe Frauen, die vor tausend Jahren
Geliebt von Dichtern und besungen waren.

Ich liebe Städte, deren leere Mauern
Königsgeschlechter alter Zeit betrauern.

Ich liebe Städte, die erstehen werden,
Wenn niemand mehr von heute lebt auf Erden.

Ich liebe Frauen — schlanke, wunderbare,
Die ungeboren ruhn im Schoss der Jahre.

Sie werden einst mit ihrer sternebleichen
Schönheit der Schönheit meiner Träume gleichen.

"I LOVE WOMEN"

I love women who a thousand years ago
Were loved by poets and in songs extolled.

I love cities whose empty walls
Bemoan the ancient royal houses.

I love cities that will rise,
When no one of today is still alive on earth.

I love women — slender, wonderful,
Who rest unborn within the womb of time.

Some day they will with their starry-pale
Beauty equal the beauty of my dreams.

Franz Werfel

(1890-1945)

Franz Werfel, like his friend Rilke, was born in Prague. One of Europe's leading authors, he also gained recognition in the United States, where he spent the last five years of his life. His novels *The Forty Days of Musa Dagh* and *The Song of Bernadette* became best sellers (the latter was also made into a successful film), while Broadway acclaimed his dramas *The Eternal Road* and *Jacobowsky and the Colonel.** It is no accident that Werfel attained more than national recognition. His attitude is always cosmopolitan; his themes of universal concern. Significantly, the first volume of his poetry, of which *An den Leser* is the poetic preamble, is entitled *Weltfreund* (Friend of the World). His poetry is thus in many ways the antithesis to that of Stefan George. Whereas George wished to write for the select few (and strongly disapproved of Werfel's attitude), the latter wanted to write for all of mankind; while George's poems are polished in form and use only the choicest vocabulary, Werfel, out of a distrust for both, frequently breaks the rhythm of his poems and includes the most common words of everyday usage. Thus in *An den Leser* he finds his inspiration in man's daily toil and draws his images from a world familiar to everyone: a child's popgun, a man bent over his ledger, a stoker firing a furnace. But the very unpretentiousness of theme, setting, and vocabulary lends a note of sincerity to Werfel's expression of empathy with the common man and his lot and to his apostrophe to all of mankind as his brethren.

* Adapted in Hollywood in 1958 as *Me and The Colonel.*

AN DEN LESER

Mein einziger Wunsch ist, Dir, oh Mensch verwandt zu sein!
Bist Du Neger, Akrobat, oder ruhst Du noch in tiefer
  Mutterhut,
Klingt Dein Mädchenlied über den Hof, lenkst
  Du Dein Floss im Abendschein,
Bist Du Soldat, oder Aviatiker voll Ausdauer und
  Mut.

Trugst Du als Kind auch ein Gewehr in grüner
  Armschlinge?
Wenn es losging, entflog ein angebundener Stöpsel dem
  Lauf.
Mein Mensch, wenn ich Erinnerung singe,
Sei nicht hart und löse Dich mit mir in Tränen auf!

Denn ich habe alle Schicksale mitgemacht: Ich weiss
Das Gefühl von einsamen Harfenistinnen in Kurkapellen,
Das Gefühl von schüchternen Gouvernanten im fremden
  Familienkreis,
Das Gefühl von Debutanten, die sich zitternd vor den
  Souffleurkasten stellen.

Ich lebte im Walde, hatte ein Bahnhofsamt,
Sass gebeugt über Kassabücher, und bediente
  ungeduldige Gäste.
Als Heizer stand ich vor Kesseln, das Antlitz grell
  überflammt,
Und als Kuli ass ich Abfall und Küchenreste.

So gehöre ich Dir und allen!
Wolle mir, bitte, nicht widerstehn!
Oh, könnte es einmal geschehn,
Dass wir uns, Bruder, in die Arme fallen!

TO THE READER

It is my sole desire, oh Man, to be related to you!
Whether you be a Negro, an acrobat, or whether you still
    repose deep in mother's care,
Whether your girlish song sounds across the courtyard,
    whether you steer your raft in the glow of evening,
Whether you are a soldier, or an aviator, full of endurance
    and courage.

Did you too, as a child, carry a gun in a green
    sling?
When it went off, a fastened cork flew from the
    barrel.
Oh, Fellow-Man, when I sing of my memories,
Be not unbending, and dissolve with me in tears!

For in all fates have I participated. I know
The feeling of lonely lady-harpists in spa-orchestras,
The feeling of shy governesses in strange family
    circles,
The feeling of debutant actors, who tremblingly stand
    close to the prompter's box.

I lived in the forest, was a railroad official,
Sat bent over ledgers and served impatient
    guests.
As a stoker I stood before boilers, my face glaringly lit
    by the flames,
And as a coolie I ate garbage and left-overs.

Thus I belonged to you and to all!
Do not, I beg, do not resist me!
Oh, if only it someday could happen,
That we, my Brother, could fall into each other's arms!

Erich Kästner
(1899-1974)

Erich Kästner, whose biting poetry will remind American readers of Ogden Nash, is a master of two distinct, almost disparate genres of literature. He has delighted millions of youngsters in all parts of the world by his children's books; his *Emil and the Detectives*, for example, has gone through countless editions and has been made into a movie several times. His adult books, on the other hand, are highly sophisticated and urbane; the bulk of his poetry, designed to satirize the foibles and vices of mankind, is bold and aggressive in subject matter and sparkles with witticisms.

Kästner's aim is to introduce a "new objectivity" into poetry. Consequently his poems, of which *Entwicklung der Menschheit* is typical, are strongly realistic; he deals with all aspects of life, from the sublime to the almost sordid. His rhyme scheme and rhythm are by choice conventional and simple; in order to be as clear and understandable as possible, Kästner rarely makes use of poetic license in the syntactical constructions of his lines. And his language, in the words of his friend and fellow-writer Hermann Kesten, is *chemisch gereinigt* (dry-cleaned); it avoids "poetic" vocabulary, lest it evoke a wealth of emotional connotations which would run counter to Kästner's rationalistic purposes. Instead, the poet has recourse to foreign derivatives, technical terms, and a scientific vocabulary.

As a result Kästner's message — and behind the wit and banter a message is always apparent — is unencumbered and becomes clear immediately. In his novel *Fabian,* Kästner expresses the conviction that modern man must undergo a moral renascence to survive. This is also the moral of *Entwicklung der Menschheit;* as in so many of Kästner's poems, the vaunted advances of man are shown up as hollow gains if contrasted with the simultaneous ethical stand-still.

DIE ENTWICKLUNG DER MENSCHHEIT

Einst haben die Kerls auf den Bäumen gehockt,
behaart und mit böser Visage.
Dann hat man sie aus dem Urwald gelockt
und die Welt asphaltiert und aufgestockt,
bis zur dreissigsten Etage.

Da sassen sie nun, den Flöhen entflohn,
in zentralgeheizten Räumen.
Da sitzen sie nun am Telephon.
Und es herrscht noch genau derselbe Ton
wie seinerzeit auf den Bäumen.

Sie hören weit. Sie sehen fern.
Sie sind mit dem Weltall in Fühlung.
Sie putzen die Zähne. Sie atmen modern.
Die Erde ist ein gebildeter Stern
mit sehr viel Wasserspülung.

Sie schiessen die Briefschaften durch ein Rohr.
Sie jagen und züchten Mikroben.
Sie versehn die Natur mit allem Komfort.
Sie fliegen steil in den Himmel empor
und bleiben zwei Wochen oben.

Was ihre Verdauung übrig lässt,
das verarbeiten sie zu Watte.
Sie spalten Atome. Sie heilen Inzest.
Und sie stellen durch Stiluntersuchungen fest,
dass Cäsar Plattfüsse hatte.

So haben sie mit dem Kopf und dem Mund
den Fortschritt der Menschheit geschaffen.
Doch davon mal abgesehen und
bei Lichte betrachtet sind sie im Grund
noch immer die alten Affen.

THE DEVELOPMENT OF MANKIND

These fellows were once squatting in trees,
all covered by hair and with a mean expression.
Then they were lured out of the forest primeval
and the world was paved and buildings constructed
up to the thirtieth story.

There they now sit, having fled from the fleas,
in rooms, centrally heated.
There they now sit at the telephone.
And there yet prevails the very same tone
as there did, back then, in the trees.

They listen to the radio. They watch T.V.
They are in touch with the universe.
They brush their teeth. Their breathing is modern.
The earth is a civilized planet
with flush toilets all over the place.

They shoot their letters via pneumatic tubes.
They hunt and breed microbes.
They endow nature with all sorts of comforts.
They fly straight up into the sky
and for two weeks remain up there.

Whatever's left over from their digestion,
they use to manufacture sterilized cotton.
They split the atom. They cure incest.
And by stylistic analysis they ascertain
that Caesar had flat feet.

Thus they have, by brain and by mouth,
created mankind's progress.
But leaving all this aside and
observed under light, they at bottom are
still the same old monkeys.

Albrecht Haushofer
(1903-1945)

In the night of April 25, 1945 — when the Russian army had already ringed Berlin — a group of fourteen political prisoners were taken from their cells in the Moabit Prison and told that they had been set free. Hardly had they crossed the prison gate into long-awaited freedom when all fourteen were brutally shot down by a detachment of SS-Guards. The next day when relatives came searching for the dead, they found among them a prisoner who held clutched in his hands a notebook with poems, the *Moabiter Sonette.* The poet was Albrecht Haushofer, a young professor at the Berlin Graduate School of Political Science who had been imprisoned for a few months as early as 1941 for daring to raise his voice against Hitler in the midst of the latter's period of greatest victories. Although Haushofer was firmly convinced that "as evil incarnate, Hitler must come to a bitter end," he sought to further Hitler's downfall more actively by participating in a resistance group which planned to assassinate the Führer. Arrested again in 1944, when the plot was uncovered, Haushofer felt that his only guilt lay in not having "realized earlier his duty of castigating more vehemently evil as evil." Throughout the *Moabiter Sonette* rings Haushofer's love of mankind and his devotion to the German people. He felt that he would have been a "criminal, had he not planned from his conscience for the tomorrow of his people."

The poem included in this selection is of special interest because it is addressed to his father, the famous Professor Karl Haushofer, whose science of geopolitics and political philosophy had a strong influence on Hitler's expansionist plans. Karl Haushofer committed suicide in 1946.

DER VATER

Ein tiefes Märchen aus dem Morgenland
erzählt uns, dass die Geister böser Macht
gefangen sitzen in des Meeres Nacht,
versiegelt von besorgter Gotteshand,

bis einmal im Jahrtausend wohl das Glück
dem einen Fischer die Entscheidung gönne,
der die Gefesselten entsiegeln könne,
wirft er den Fund nicht gleich ins Meer zurück.

Für meinen Vater war das Los gesprochen.
Es lag einmal in seines Willens Kraft,
den Dämon heimzustossen in die Haft.

Mein Vater hat das Siegel aufgebrochen.
Den Hauch des Bösen hat er nicht gesehn.
Den Dämon liess er in die Welt entwehn.

THE FATHER

A tale profound from Eastern lands
narrates to us that spirits of foul power
rest captured in the ocean's night,
sealed up by anxious hands of God,

until just once in a millennium, a chance
grants to a fisher the decision,
who could unseal the fettered spirits
if he at once not cast back his find into the sea.

This chance was given to my father.
It once reposed within the power of his will
to push the demon back into confinement.

The seal my father did break open.
He did not see the breath of evil.
He let the demon drift into the night.

Bertolt Brecht

(1898-1956)

Brecht's fame has been firmly established by the sensational international success of the musical play *The Threepenny Opera* (the brilliant score is by Kurt Weill). Since 1928 this corrosively funny satire on the rottenness of bourgeois morality and soulless utilitarianism has delighted audiences in Berlin, New York, Paris, and London. But Brecht is even more eminent as the originator of a new theory of the drama, the Epic Theater, and as the creator of his own company, the Berlin Ensemble, whose performances of his plays *Mother Courage, The Good Woman of Setzuan,* and *Galileo* have won wide acclaim in Germany, London, and Paris.

One of the most gifted, original, and controversial German poets, Brecht's often devastating poetic vigor sprang from an urge to social protest marked by leftist, if not Communist, leanings. After years of political exile from Nazi Germany he returned to East Germany to become one of its leading cultural spokesmen. Shortly before his death he seems, however, to have run into political trouble. Although his opera *Lukullus* received a standing ovation on the opening night, it was withdrawn only to reappear purged of its utter and absolute condemnation of all war; new lines proclaimed a defensive war as an acceptable, indeed even noble enterprise.

As a poet, Brecht excelled in adapting the down-to-earth sauciness of ballads and folksongs and in formulating snarling and catching lines whose acid humor is never quite free from despair. And always, beneath the political and cynical Brecht, there is the inner man, the humanist Brecht who believes that man is naturally good, that he must make an effort to be evil, as he proclaims in his revealing poem, *Mask of Evil*. For man, he observes both cynically and despairingly in *The Threepenny Opera*, would like to be good, "but circumstance won't have it so."

The same note of agonized hopefulness in the midst of de-humanized existence appears in the original *(Hauspostille-)* version of the poem "On the Friendliness of the World": the world may be cold and cruel, but: "Perhaps, my friend, you did not matter to a lot of people. But many others wept over you, too."

Brecht, the ruthless and cynical unmasker of life with a soft spot in his heart, is also apparent in "Recollection of Marie A." At first this is just one more sentimental elegy on young and lost love. But abruptly the poet jolts us with a characteristic Brechtian twist: his coldly cynical confession that he cannot remember what love is nor the face of the girl. (Or has he suppressed it because the thought of her now being a dowdy matron with seven children would spoil his memory?) Even the kiss would be long forgotten were it not for that cloud, "so very white and so immensely lofty." Yet beneath this pose of oddly-combined sentimentality and cynicism, we sense the deeper Brecht, the human being and poet, whose image of the cloud, winging its way over the transitory, lends permanence and lasting beauty to the recollection of Marie A.

Both Brecht poems for this anthology were selected by Lotte Lenya, who together with her husband, Kurt Weill, knew the poet well during every stage of his literary career.

ERINNERUNG AN DIE MARIE A.

1

An jenem Tag im blauen Mond September
Still unter einem jungen Pflaumenbaum
Da hielt ich sie, die stille bleiche Liebe
In meinem Arm wie einen holden Traum.
Und über uns im schönen Sommerhimmel
War eine Wolke, die ich lange sah
Sie war sehr weiss und ungeheuer oben
Und als ich aufsah, war sie nimmer da.

2

Seit jenem Tag sind viele, viele Monde
Geschwommen still hinunter und vorbei.
Die Pflaumenbäume sind wohl abgehauen
Und fragst du mich was mit der Liebe sei?
So sag ich dir: Ich kann mich nicht erinnern
Und doch, gewiss, ich weiss schon, was du meinst.
Doch ihr Gesicht, das weiss ich wirklich nimmer
Ich weiss nur mehr: Ich küsste es dereinst.

3

Und auch den Kuss, ich hätt' ihn längst vergessen
Wenn nicht die Wolke dagewesen wär
Die weiss ich noch und werd ich immer wissen
Sie war sehr weiss und kam von oben her.
Die Pflaumenbäume blühn vielleicht noch immer
Und jene Frau hat jetzt vielleicht das siebte Kind
Doch jene Wolke blühte nur Minuten
Und als ich aufsah, schwand sie schon im Wind.

RECOLLECTION OF MARIE A.

1

Upon that day in the clear-skied month September
Beneath a sapling plum tree, quietly
I held her there, my quiet, wan beloved one
Within my arms just like a lovely dream.
And over us in the fair sky of the summer
There was a cloud on which I gazed for long
It was so very white and so immensely lofty
And when I looked up, it was gone.

2

Since that day so many, many months
Have floated down and floated past.
The plum trees probably were felled
And if you ask me what's become of love?
I'll answer you: I cannot recall
And yet it's certain I do know what you mean.
But, truly, I no longer can recall her face
I just recall: I kissed it then.

3

And that kiss too I would have long ago forgotten
Had not the cloud been present there
That I recall and always will recall it
It was so white and came from high above.
Perhaps those plum trees still bear blossoms
And that woman now may have her seventh child
That cloud, however, blossomed just for minutes
And when I gazed up, faded in the wind.

VON DER FREUNDLICHKEIT DER WELT

1

Auf die Erde voller kaltem Wind
Kamt ihr alle als ein nacktes Kind.
Frierend lagt ihr ohne alle Hab
Als ein Weib euch eine Windel gab.

2

Keiner schrie euch, ihr wart nicht begehrt
Und man holte euch nicht im Gefährt.
Hier auf Erden wart ihr unbekannt
Als ein Mann euch einst nahm an der Hand.

3

Und die Welt, die ist euch gar nichts schuld:
Keiner hält euch, wenn ihr gehen wollt.
Vielen, Kinder, wart ihr vielleicht gleich.
Viele aber weinten über euch.

4

Von der Erde voller kaltem Wind
Geht ihr all bedeckt mit Schorf und Grind.
Fast ein jeder hat die Welt geliebt
Wenn man ihm zwei Hände Erde gibt.

ON THE WORLD'S FRIENDLINESS

1

Unto this earth full of cold winds
You each came as a naked child.
Freezing, you lay without the least possession
When some woman gave you swaddling clothes.

2

To you called no one, no one wanted you
And people did not fetch you in a fancy carriage.
Upon this earth you were unknown,
When some man took you by the hand.

3

And the world, it doesn't owe you anything:
If you want to leave it, no one will hold you back.
Perhaps, my friend, you did not matter to a lot of people.
But many others wept over you, too.

4

Away from earth, full of cold winds
You all depart begrimed with scab and filth.
Almost each one has loved this world
When two handfuls of earth are given him.

A CATALOG OF SELECTED
DOVER BOOKS
IN ALL FIELDS OF INTEREST

A CATALOG OF SELECTED DOVER
BOOKS IN ALL FIELDS OF INTEREST

CONCERNING THE SPIRITUAL IN ART, Wassily Kandinsky. Pioneering work by father of abstract art. Thoughts on color theory, nature of art. Analysis of earlier masters. 12 illustrations. 80pp. of text. 5⅜ x 8½. 23411-8 Pa. $3.95

ANIMALS: 1,419 Copyright-Free Illustrations of Mammals, Birds, Fish, Insects, etc., Jim Harter (ed.). Clear wood engravings present, in extremely lifelike poses, over 1,000 species of animals. One of the most extensive pictorial sourcebooks of its kind. Captions. Index. 284pp. 9 x 12. 23766-4 Pa. $12.95

CELTIC ART: The Methods of Construction, George Bain. Simple geometric techniques for making Celtic interlacements, spirals, Kells-type initials, animals, humans, etc. Over 500 illustrations. 160pp. 9 x 12. (USO) 22923-8 Pa. $9.95

AN ATLAS OF ANATOMY FOR ARTISTS, Fritz Schider. Most thorough reference work on art anatomy in the world. Hundreds of illustrations, including selections from works by Vesalius, Leonardo, Goya, Ingres, Michelangelo, others. 593 illustrations. 192pp. 7⅛ x 10¼. 20241-0 Pa. $9.95

CELTIC HAND STROKE-BY-STROKE (Irish Half-Uncial from "The Book of Kells"): An Arthur Baker Calligraphy Manual, Arthur Baker. Complete guide to creating each letter of the alphabet in distinctive Celtic manner. Covers hand position, strokes, pens, inks, paper, more. Illustrated. 48pp. 8¼ x 11. 24336-2 Pa. $3.95

EASY ORIGAMI, John Montroll. Charming collection of 32 projects (hat, cup, pelican, piano, swan, many more) specially designed for the novice origami hobbyist. Clearly illustrated easy-to-follow instructions insure that even beginning papercrafters will achieve successful results. 48pp. 8¼ x 11. 27298-2 Pa. $3.50

THE COMPLETE BOOK OF BIRDHOUSE CONSTRUCTION FOR WOOD-WORKERS, Scott D. Campbell. Detailed instructions, illustrations, tables. Also data on bird habitat and instinct patterns. Bibliography. 3 tables. 63 illustrations in 15 figures. 48pp. 5¼ x 8½. 24407-5 Pa. $2.50

BLOOMINGDALE'S ILLUSTRATED 1886 CATALOG: Fashions, Dry Goods and Housewares, Bloomingdale Brothers. Famed merchants' extremely rare catalog depicting about 1,700 products: clothing, housewares, firearms, dry goods, jewelry, more. Invaluable for dating, identifying vintage items. Also, copyright-free graphics for artists, designers. Co-published with Henry Ford Museum & Greenfield Village. 160pp. 8¼ x 11. 25780-0 Pa. $10.95

HISTORIC COSTUME IN PICTURES, Braun & Schneider. Over 1,450 costumed figures in clearly detailed engravings–from dawn of civilization to end of 19th century. Captions. Many folk costumes. 256pp. 8⅜ x 11¾. 23150-X Pa. $12.95

STICKLEY CRAFTSMAN FURNITURE CATALOGS, Gustav Stickley and L. & J. G. Stickley. Beautiful, functional furniture in two authentic catalogs from 1910. 594 illustrations, including 277 photos, show settles, rockers, armchairs, reclining chairs, bookcases, desks, tables. 183pp. 6½ x 9¼.   23838-5 Pa. $9.95

AMERICAN LOCOMOTIVES IN HISTORIC PHOTOGRAPHS: 1858 to 1949, Ron Ziel (ed.). A rare collection of 126 meticulously detailed official photographs, called "builder portraits," of American locomotives that majestically chronicle the rise of steam locomotive power in America. Introduction. Detailed captions. xi + 129pp. 9 x 12.   27393-8 Pa. $12.95

AMERICA'S LIGHTHOUSES: An Illustrated History, Francis Ross Holland, Jr. Delightfully written, profusely illustrated fact-filled survey of over 200 American lighthouses since 1716. History, anecdotes, technological advances, more. 240pp. 8 x 10¾.
                                              25576-X Pa. $12.95

TOWARDS A NEW ARCHITECTURE, Le Corbusier. Pioneering manifesto by founder of "International School." Technical and aesthetic theories, views of industry, economics, relation of form to function, "mass-production split" and much more. Profusely illustrated. 320pp. 6⅛ x 9¼. (USO)   25023-7 Pa. $9.95

HOW THE OTHER HALF LIVES, Jacob Riis. Famous journalistic record, exposing poverty and degradation of New York slums around 1900, by major social reformer. 100 striking and influential photographs. 233pp. 10 x 7⅞.
                                                22012-5 Pa. $10.95

FRUIT KEY AND TWIG KEY TO TREES AND SHRUBS, William M. Harlow. One of the handiest and most widely used identification aids. Fruit key covers 120 deciduous and evergreen species; twig key 160 deciduous species. Easily used. Over 300 photographs. 126pp. 5⅜ x 8½.   20511-8 Pa. $3.95

COMMON BIRD SONGS, Dr. Donald J. Borror. Songs of 60 most common U.S. birds: robins, sparrows, cardinals, bluejays, finches, more—arranged in order of increasing complexity. Up to 9 variations of songs of each species.
                                   Cassette and manual 99911-4 $8.95

ORCHIDS AS HOUSE PLANTS, Rebecca Tyson Northen. Grow cattleyas and many other kinds of orchids—in a window, in a case, or under artificial light. 63 illustrations. 148pp. 5⅜ x 8½.   23261-1 Pa. $4.95

MONSTER MAZES, Dave Phillips. Masterful mazes at four levels of difficulty. Avoid deadly perils and evil creatures to find magical treasures. Solutions for all 32 exciting illustrated puzzles. 48pp. 8¼ x 11.   26005-4 Pa. $2.95

MOZART'S DON GIOVANNI (DOVER OPERA LIBRETTO SERIES), Wolfgang Amadeus Mozart. Introduced and translated by Ellen H. Bleiler. Standard Italian libretto, with complete English translation. Convenient and thoroughly portable—an ideal companion for reading along with a recording or the performance itself. Introduction. List of characters. Plot summary. 121pp. 5¼ x 8½.
                                                24944-1 Pa. $2.95

TECHNICAL MANUAL AND DICTIONARY OF CLASSICAL BALLET, Gail Grant. Defines, explains, comments on steps, movements, poses and concepts. 15-page pictorial section. Basic book for student, viewer. 127pp. 5⅜ x 8½.
                                                21843-0 Pa. $4.95

BRASS INSTRUMENTS: Their History and Development, Anthony Baines. Authoritative, updated survey of the evolution of trumpets, trombones, bugles, cornets, French horns, tubas and other brass wind instruments. Over 140 illustrations and 48 music examples. Corrected and updated by author. New preface. Bibliography. 320pp. 5⅜ x 8½. 27574-4 Pa. $9.95

HOLLYWOOD GLAMOR PORTRAITS, John Kobal (ed.). 145 photos from 1926-49. Harlow, Gable, Bogart, Bacall; 94 stars in all. Full background on photographers, technical aspects. 160pp. 8⅜ x 11¼. 23352-9 Pa. $12.95

MAX AND MORITZ, Wilhelm Busch. Great humor classic in both German and English. Also 10 other works: "Cat and Mouse," "Plisch and Plumm," etc. 216pp. 5⅜ x 8½. 20181-3 Pa. $6.95

THE RAVEN AND OTHER FAVORITE POEMS, Edgar Allan Poe. Over 40 of the author's most memorable poems: "The Bells," "Ulalume," "Israfel," "To Helen," "The Conqueror Worm," "Eldorado," "Annabel Lee," many more. Alphabetic lists of titles and first lines. 64pp. 5³⁄₁₆ x 8¼. 26685-0 Pa. $1.00

PERSONAL MEMOIRS OF U. S. GRANT, Ulysses Simpson Grant. Intelligent, deeply moving firsthand account of Civil War campaigns, considered by many the finest military memoirs ever written. Includes letters, historic photographs, maps and more. 528pp. 6⅛ x 9¼. 28587-1 Pa. $11.95

AMULETS AND SUPERSTITIONS, E. A. Wallis Budge. Comprehensive discourse on origin, powers of amulets in many ancient cultures: Arab, Persian Babylonian, Assyrian, Egyptian, Gnostic, Hebrew, Phoenician, Syriac, etc. Covers cross, swastika, crucifix, seals, rings, stones, etc. 584pp. 5⅜ x 8½. 23573-4 Pa. $12.95

RUSSIAN STORIES/PYCCKNE PACCKA3bl: A Dual-Language Book, edited by Gleb Struve. Twelve tales by such masters as Chekhov, Tolstoy, Dostoevsky, Pushkin, others. Excellent word-for-word English translations on facing pages, plus teaching and study aids, Russian/English vocabulary, biographical/critical introductions, more. 416pp. 5⅜ x 8½. 26244-8 Pa. $8.95

PHILADELPHIA THEN AND NOW: 60 Sites Photographed in the Past and Present, Kenneth Finkel and Susan Oyama. Rare photographs of City Hall, Logan Square, Independence Hall, Betsy Ross House, other landmarks juxtaposed with contemporary views. Captures changing face of historic city. Introduction. Captions. 128pp. 8¼ x 11. 25790-8 Pa. $9.95

AIA ARCHITECTURAL GUIDE TO NASSAU AND SUFFOLK COUNTIES, LONG ISLAND, The American Institute of Architects, Long Island Chapter, and the Society for the Preservation of Long Island Antiquities. Comprehensive, well-researched and generously illustrated volume brings to life over three centuries of Long Island's great architectural heritage. More than 240 photographs with authoritative, extensively detailed captions. 176pp. 8¼ x 11. 26946-9 Pa. $14.95

NORTH AMERICAN INDIAN LIFE: Customs and Traditions of 23 Tribes, Elsie Clews Parsons (ed.). 27 fictionalized essays by noted anthropologists examine religion, customs, government, additional facets of life among the Winnebago, Crow, Zuni, Eskimo, other tribes. 480pp. 6⅛ x 9¼. 27377-6 Pa. $10.95

FRANK LLOYD WRIGHT'S HOLLYHOCK HOUSE, Donald Hoffmann. Lavishly illustrated, carefully documented study of one of Wright's most controversial residential designs. Over 120 photographs, floor plans, elevations, etc. Detailed perceptive text by noted Wright scholar. Index. 128pp. 9¼ x 10¾. 27133-1 Pa. $11.95

THE MALE AND FEMALE FIGURE IN MOTION: 60 Classic Photographic Sequences, Eadweard Muybridge. 60 true-action photographs of men and women walking, running, climbing, bending, turning, etc., reproduced from rare 19th-century masterpiece. vi + 121pp. 9 x 12. 24745-7 Pa. $10.95

1001 QUESTIONS ANSWERED ABOUT THE SEASHORE, N. J. Berrill and Jacquelyn Berrill. Queries answered about dolphins, sea snails, sponges, starfish, fishes, shore birds, many others. Covers appearance, breeding, growth, feeding, much more. 305pp. 5¼ x 8¼. 23366-9 Pa. $8.95

GUIDE TO OWL WATCHING IN NORTH AMERICA, Donald S. Heintzelman. Superb guide offers complete data and descriptions of 19 species: barn owl, screech owl, snowy owl, many more. Expert coverage of owl-watching equipment, conservation, migrations and invasions, etc. Guide to observing sites. 84 illustrations. xiii + 193pp. 5⅜ x 8½. 27344-X Pa. $8.95

MEDICINAL AND OTHER USES OF NORTH AMERICAN PLANTS: A Historical Survey with Special Reference to the Eastern Indian Tribes, Charlotte Erichsen-Brown. Chronological historical citations document 500 years of usage of plants, trees, shrubs native to eastern Canada, northeastern U.S. Also complete identifying information. 343 illustrations. 544pp. 6½ x 9¼. 25951-X Pa. $12.95

STORYBOOK MAZES, Dave Phillips. 23 stories and mazes on two-page spreads: Wizard of Oz, Treasure Island, Robin Hood, etc. Solutions. 64pp. 8¼ x 11. 23628-5 Pa. $2.95

NEGRO FOLK MUSIC, U.S.A., Harold Courlander. Noted folklorist's scholarly yet readable analysis of rich and varied musical tradition. Includes authentic versions of over 40 folk songs. Valuable bibliography and discography. xi + 324pp. 5⅜ x 8½. 27350-4 Pa. $9.95

MOVIE-STAR PORTRAITS OF THE FORTIES, John Kobal (ed.). 163 glamor, studio photos of 106 stars of the 1940s: Rita Hayworth, Ava Gardner, Marlon Brando, Clark Gable, many more. 176pp. 8⅜ x 11¼. 23546-7 Pa. $12.95

BENCHLEY LOST AND FOUND, Robert Benchley. Finest humor from early 30s, about pet peeves, child psychologists, post office and others. Mostly unavailable elsewhere. 73 illustrations by Peter Arno and others. 183pp. 5⅜ x 8½. 22410-4 Pa. $6.95

YEKL and THE IMPORTED BRIDEGROOM AND OTHER STORIES OF YIDDISH NEW YORK, Abraham Cahan. Film Hester Street based on Yekl (1896). Novel, other stories among first about Jewish immigrants on N.Y.'s East Side. 240pp. 5⅜ x 8½. 22427-9 Pa. $6.95

SELECTED POEMS, Walt Whitman. Generous sampling from *Leaves of Grass*. Twenty-four poems include "I Hear America Singing," "Song of the Open Road," "I Sing the Body Electric," "When Lilacs Last in the Dooryard Bloom'd," "O Captain! My Captain!"—all reprinted from an authoritative edition. Lists of titles and first lines. 128pp. 5³⁄₁₆ x 8¼. 26878-0 Pa. $1.00

THE BEST TALES OF HOFFMANN, E. T. A. Hoffmann. 10 of Hoffmann's most important stories: "Nutcracker and the King of Mice," "The Golden Flowerpot," etc. 458pp. 5⅜ x 8½. 21793-0 Pa. $9.95

FROM FETISH TO GOD IN ANCIENT EGYPT, E. A. Wallis Budge. Rich detailed survey of Egyptian conception of "God" and gods, magic, cult of animals, Osiris, more. Also, superb English translations of hymns and legends. 240 illustrations. 545pp. 5⅜ x 8½. 25803-3 Pa. $13.95

FRENCH STORIES/CONTES FRANÇAIS: A Dual-Language Book, Wallace Fowlie. Ten stories by French masters, Voltaire to Camus: "Micromegas" by Voltaire; "The Atheist's Mass" by Balzac; "Minuet" by de Maupassant; "The Guest" by Camus, six more. Excellent English translations on facing pages. Also French-English vocabulary list, exercises, more. 352pp. 5⅜ x 8½. 26443-2 Pa. $8.95

CHICAGO AT THE TURN OF THE CENTURY IN PHOTOGRAPHS: 122 Historic Views from the Collections of the Chicago Historical Society, Larry A. Viskochil. Rare large-format prints offer detailed views of City Hall, State Street, the Loop, Hull House, Union Station, many other landmarks, circa 1904-1913. Introduction. Captions. Maps. 144pp. 9⅜ x 12¼. 24656-6 Pa. $12.95

OLD BROOKLYN IN EARLY PHOTOGRAPHS, 1865-1929, William Lee Younger. Luna Park, Gravesend race track, construction of Grand Army Plaza, moving of Hotel Brighton, etc. 157 previously unpublished photographs. 165pp. 8⅞ x 11¾. 23587-4 Pa. $13.95

THE MYTHS OF THE NORTH AMERICAN INDIANS, Lewis Spence. Rich anthology of the myths and legends of the Algonquins, Iroquois, Pawnees and Sioux, prefaced by an extensive historical and ethnological commentary. 36 illustrations. 480pp. 5⅜ x 8½. 25967-6 Pa. $8.95

AN ENCYCLOPEDIA OF BATTLES: Accounts of Over 1,560 Battles from 1479 B.C. to the Present, David Eggenberger. Essential details of every major battle in recorded history from the first battle of Megiddo in 1479 B.C. to Grenada in 1984. List of Battle Maps. New Appendix covering the years 1967-1984. Index. 99 illustrations. 544pp. 6½ x 9¼. 24913-1 Pa. $14.95

SAILING ALONE AROUND THE WORLD, Captain Joshua Slocum. First man to sail around the world, alone, in small boat. One of great feats of seamanship told in delightful manner. 67 illustrations. 294pp. 5⅜ x 8½. 20326-3 Pa. $5.95

ANARCHISM AND OTHER ESSAYS, Emma Goldman. Powerful, penetrating, prophetic essays on direct action, role of minorities, prison reform, puritan hypocrisy, violence, etc. 271pp. 5⅜ x 8½. 22484-8 Pa. $6.95

MYTHS OF THE HINDUS AND BUDDHISTS, Ananda K. Coomaraswamy and Sister Nivedita. Great stories of the epics; deeds of Krishna, Shiva, taken from puranas, Vedas, folk tales; etc. 32 illustrations. 400pp. 5⅜ x 8½. 21759-0 Pa. $10.95

BEYOND PSYCHOLOGY, Otto Rank. Fear of death, desire of immortality, nature of sexuality, social organization, creativity, according to Rankian system. 291pp. 5⅜ x 8½. 20485-5 Pa. $8.95

A THEOLOGICO-POLITICAL TREATISE, Benedict Spinoza. Also contains unfinished Political Treatise. Great classic on religious liberty, theory of government on common consent. R. Elwes translation. Total of 421pp. 5⅜ x 8½. 20249-6 Pa. $9.95

MY BONDAGE AND MY FREEDOM, Frederick Douglass. Born a slave, Douglass became outspoken force in antislavery movement. The best of Douglass' autobiographies. Graphic description of slave life. 464pp. 5⅜ x 8½. 22457-0 Pa. $8.95

FOLLOWING THE EQUATOR: A Journey Around the World, Mark Twain. Fascinating humorous account of 1897 voyage to Hawaii, Australia, India, New Zealand, etc. Ironic, bemused reports on peoples, customs, climate, flora and fauna, politics, much more. 197 illustrations. 720pp. 5⅜ x 8½. 26113-1 Pa. $15.95

THE PEOPLE CALLED SHAKERS, Edward D. Andrews. Definitive study of Shakers: origins, beliefs, practices, dances, social organization, furniture and crafts, etc. 33 illustrations. 351pp. 5⅜ x 8½. 21081-2 Pa. $8.95

THE MYTHS OF GREECE AND ROME, H. A. Guerber. A classic of mythology, generously illustrated, long prized for its simple, graphic, accurate retelling of the principal myths of Greece and Rome, and for its commentary on their origins and significance. With 64 illustrations by Michelangelo, Raphael, Titian, Rubens, Canova, Bernini and others. 480pp. 5⅜ x 8½. 27584-1 Pa. $9.95

PSYCHOLOGY OF MUSIC, Carl E. Seashore. Classic work discusses music as a medium from psychological viewpoint. Clear treatment of physical acoustics, auditory apparatus, sound perception, development of musical skills, nature of musical feeling, host of other topics. 88 figures. 408pp. 5⅜ x 8½. 21851-1 Pa. $10.95

THE PHILOSOPHY OF HISTORY, Georg W. Hegel. Great classic of Western thought develops concept that history is not chance but rational process, the evolution of freedom. 457pp. 5⅜ x 8½. 20112-0 Pa. $9.95

THE BOOK OF TEA, Kakuzo Okakura. Minor classic of the Orient: entertaining, charming explanation, interpretation of traditional Japanese culture in terms of tea ceremony. 94pp. 5⅜ x 8½. 20070-1 Pa. $3.95

LIFE IN ANCIENT EGYPT, Adolf Erman. Fullest, most thorough, detailed older account with much not in more recent books, domestic life, religion, magic, medicine, commerce, much more. Many illustrations reproduce tomb paintings, carvings, hieroglyphs, etc. 597pp. 5⅜ x 8½. 22632-8 Pa. $11.95

SUNDIALS, Their Theory and Construction, Albert Waugh. Far and away the best, most thorough coverage of ideas, mathematics concerned, types, construction, adjusting anywhere. Simple, nontechnical treatment allows even children to build several of these dials. Over 100 illustrations. 230pp. 5⅜ x 8½. 22947-5 Pa. $7.95

DYNAMICS OF FLUIDS IN POROUS MEDIA, Jacob Bear. For advanced students of ground water hydrology, soil mechanics and physics, drainage and irrigation engineering, and more. 335 illustrations. Exercises, with answers. 784pp. 6⅛ x 9¼. 65675-6 Pa. $19.95

SONGS OF EXPERIENCE: Facsimile Reproduction with 26 Plates in Full Color, William Blake. 26 full-color plates from a rare 1826 edition. Includes "The Tyger," "London," "Holy Thursday," and other poems. Printed text of poems. 48pp. 5¼ x 7. 24636-1 Pa. $4.95

OLD-TIME VIGNETTES IN FULL COLOR, Carol Belanger Grafton (ed.). Over 390 charming, often sentimental illustrations, selected from archives of Victorian graphics—pretty women posing, children playing, food, flowers, kittens and puppies, smiling cherubs, birds and butterflies, much more. All copyright-free. 48pp. 9¼ x 12¼. 27269-9 Pa. $7.95

PERSPECTIVE FOR ARTISTS, Rex Vicat Cole. Depth, perspective of sky and sea, shadows, much more, not usually covered. 391 diagrams, 81 reproductions of drawings and paintings. 279pp. 5⅜ x 8½. 22487-2 Pa. $7.95

DRAWING THE LIVING FIGURE, Joseph Sheppard. Innovative approach to artistic anatomy focuses on specifics of surface anatomy, rather than muscles and bones. Over 170 drawings of live models in front, back and side views, and in widely varying poses. Accompanying diagrams. 177 illustrations. Introduction. Index. 144pp. 8⅜ x11¼. 26723-7 Pa. $8.95

GOTHIC AND OLD ENGLISH ALPHABETS: 100 Complete Fonts, Dan X. Solo. Add power, elegance to posters, signs, other graphics with 100 stunning copyright-free alphabets: Blackstone, Dolbey, Germania, 97 more–including many lower-case, numerals, punctuation marks. 104pp. 8⅛ x 11. 24695-7 Pa. $8.95

HOW TO DO BEADWORK, Mary White. Fundamental book on craft from simple projects to five-bead chains and woven works. 106 illustrations. 142pp. 5⅜ x 8. 20697-1 Pa. $4.95

THE BOOK OF WOOD CARVING, Charles Marshall Sayers. Finest book for beginners discusses fundamentals and offers 34 designs. "Absolutely first rate . . . well thought out and well executed."–E. J. Tangerman. 118pp. 7¾ x 10⅝. 23654-4 Pa. $6.95

ILLUSTRATED CATALOG OF CIVIL WAR MILITARY GOODS: Union Army Weapons, Insignia, Uniform Accessories, and Other Equipment, Schuyler, Hartley, and Graham. Rare, profusely illustrated 1846 catalog includes Union Army uniform and dress regulations, arms and ammunition, coats, insignia, flags, swords, rifles, etc. 226 illustrations. 160pp. 9 x 12. 24939-5 Pa. $10.95

WOMEN'S FASHIONS OF THE EARLY 1900s: An Unabridged Republication of "New York Fashions, 1909," National Cloak & Suit Co. Rare catalog of mail-order fashions documents women's and children's clothing styles shortly after the turn of the century. Captions offer full descriptions, prices. Invaluable resource for fashion, costume historians. Approximately 725 illustrations. 128pp. 8⅜ x 11¼. 27276-1 Pa. $11.95

THE 1912 AND 1915 GUSTAV STICKLEY FURNITURE CATALOGS, Gustav Stickley. With over 200 detailed illustrations and descriptions, these two catalogs are essential reading and reference materials and identification guides for Stickley furniture. Captions cite materials, dimensions and prices. 112pp. 6½ x 9¼. 26676-1 Pa. $9.95

EARLY AMERICAN LOCOMOTIVES, John H. White, Jr. Finest locomotive engravings from early 19th century: historical (1804–74), main-line (after 1870), special, foreign, etc. 147 plates. 142pp. 11⅜ x 8¼. 22772-3 Pa. $10.95

THE TALL SHIPS OF TODAY IN PHOTOGRAPHS, Frank O. Braynard. Lavishly illustrated tribute to nearly 100 majestic contemporary sailing vessels: Amerigo Vespucci, Clearwater, Constitution, Eagle, Mayflower, Sea Cloud, Victory, many more. Authoritative captions provide statistics, background on each ship. 190 black-and-white photographs and illustrations. Introduction. 128pp. 8⅞ x 11¾. 27163-3 Pa. $13.95

EARLY NINETEENTH-CENTURY CRAFTS AND TRADES, Peter Stockham (ed.). Extremely rare 1807 volume describes to youngsters the crafts and trades of the day: brickmaker, weaver, dressmaker, bookbinder, ropemaker, saddler, many more. Quaint prose, charming illustrations for each craft. 20 black-and-white line illustrations. 192pp. 4⅝ x 6.
27293-1 Pa. $4.95

VICTORIAN FASHIONS AND COSTUMES FROM HARPER'S BAZAR, 1867–1898, Stella Blum (ed.). Day costumes, evening wear, sports clothes, shoes, hats, other accessories in over 1,000 detailed engravings. 320pp. 9⅜ x 12¼.
22990-4 Pa. $14.95

GUSTAV STICKLEY, THE CRAFTSMAN, Mary Ann Smith. Superb study surveys broad scope of Stickley's achievement, especially in architecture. Design philosophy, rise and fall of the Craftsman empire, descriptions and floor plans for many Craftsman houses, more. 86 black-and-white halftones. 31 line illustrations. Introduction 208pp. 6½ x 9¼.
27210-9 Pa. $9.95

THE LONG ISLAND RAIL ROAD IN EARLY PHOTOGRAPHS, Ron Ziel. Over 220 rare photos, informative text document origin (1844) and development of rail service on Long Island. Vintage views of early trains, locomotives, stations, passengers, crews, much more. Captions. 8⅞ x 11¾.
26301-0 Pa. $13.95

THE BOOK OF OLD SHIPS: From Egyptian Galleys to Clipper Ships, Henry B. Culver. Superb, authoritative history of sailing vessels, with 80 magnificent line illustrations. Galley, bark, caravel, longship, whaler, many more. Detailed, informative text on each vessel by noted naval historian. Introduction. 256pp. 5⅜ x 8½.
27332-6 Pa. $7.95

TEN BOOKS ON ARCHITECTURE, Vitruvius. The most important book ever written on architecture. Early Roman aesthetics, technology, classical orders, site selection, all other aspects. Morgan translation. 331pp. 5⅜ x 8½.   20645-9 Pa. $8.95

THE HUMAN FIGURE IN MOTION, Eadweard Muybridge. More than 4,500 stopped-action photos, in action series, showing undraped men, women, children jumping, lying down, throwing, sitting, wrestling, carrying, etc. 390pp. 7⅞ x 10⅝.
20204-6 Clothbd. $25.95

TREES OF THE EASTERN AND CENTRAL UNITED STATES AND CANADA, William M. Harlow. Best one-volume guide to 140 trees. Full descriptions, woodlore, range, etc. Over 600 illustrations. Handy size. 288pp. 4½ x 6⅜.
20395-6 Pa. $6.95

SONGS OF WESTERN BIRDS, Dr. Donald J. Borror. Complete song and call repertoire of 60 western species, including flycatchers, juncoes, cactus wrens, many more–includes fully illustrated booklet.   Cassette and manual 99913-0 $8.95

GROWING AND USING HERBS AND SPICES, Milo Miloradovich. Versatile handbook provides all the information needed for cultivation and use of all the herbs and spices available in North America. 4 illustrations. Index. Glossary. 236pp. 5⅜ x 8½.
25058-X Pa. $6.95

BIG BOOK OF MAZES AND LABYRINTHS, Walter Shepherd. 50 mazes and labyrinths in all–classical, solid, ripple, and more–in one great volume. Perfect inexpensive puzzler for clever youngsters. Full solutions. 112pp. 8⅛ x 11.
22951-3 Pa. $4.95

PIANO TUNING, J. Cree Fischer. Clearest, best book for beginner, amateur. Simple repairs, raising dropped notes, tuning by easy method of flattened fifths. No previous skills needed. 4 illustrations. 201pp. 5⅜ x 8½. 23267-0 Pa. $6.95

A SOURCE BOOK IN THEATRICAL HISTORY, A. M. Nagler. Contemporary observers on acting, directing, make-up, costuming, stage props, machinery, scene design, from Ancient Greece to Chekhov. 611pp. 5⅜ x 8½. 20515-0 Pa. $12.95

THE COMPLETE NONSENSE OF EDWARD LEAR, Edward Lear. All nonsense limericks, zany alphabets, Owl and Pussycat, songs, nonsense botany, etc., illustrated by Lear. Total of 320pp. 5⅜ x 8½. (USO) 20167-8 Pa. $6.95

VICTORIAN PARLOUR POETRY: An Annotated Anthology, Michael R. Turner. 117 gems by Longfellow, Tennyson, Browning, many lesser-known poets. "The Village Blacksmith," "Curfew Must Not Ring Tonight," "Only a Baby Small," dozens more, often difficult to find elsewhere. Index of poets, titles, first lines. xxiii + 325pp. 5⅝ x 8¼. 27044-0 Pa. $8.95

DUBLINERS, James Joyce. Fifteen stories offer vivid, tightly focused observations of the lives of Dublin's poorer classes. At least one, "The Dead," is considered a masterpiece. Reprinted complete and unabridged from standard edition. 160pp. 5³⁄₁₆ x 8¼. 26870-5 Pa. $1.00

THE HAUNTED MONASTERY and THE CHINESE MAZE MURDERS, Robert van Gulik. Two full novels by van Gulik, set in 7th-century China, continue adventures of Judge Dee and his companions. An evil Taoist monastery, seemingly supernatural events; overgrown topiary maze hides strange crimes. 27 illustrations. 328pp. 5⅜ x 8½. 23502-5 Pa. $8.95

THE BOOK OF THE SACRED MAGIC OF ABRAMELIN THE MAGE, translated by S. MacGregor Mathers. Medieval manuscript of ceremonial magic. Basic document in Aleister Crowley, Golden Dawn groups. 268pp. 5⅜ x 8½. 23211-5 Pa. $8.95

NEW RUSSIAN-ENGLISH AND ENGLISH-RUSSIAN DICTIONARY, M. A. O'Brien. This is a remarkably handy Russian dictionary, containing a surprising amount of information, including over 70,000 entries. 366pp. 4½ x 6⅛. 20208-9 Pa. $9.95

HISTORIC HOMES OF THE AMERICAN PRESIDENTS, Second, Revised Edition, Irvin Haas. A traveler's guide to American Presidential homes, most open to the public, depicting and describing homes occupied by every American President from George Washington to George Bush. With visiting hours, admission charges, travel routes. 175 photographs. Index. 160pp. 8¼ x 11. 26751-2 Pa. $11.95

NEW YORK IN THE FORTIES, Andreas Feininger. 162 brilliant photographs by the well-known photographer, formerly with *Life* magazine. Commuters, shoppers, Times Square at night, much else from city at its peak. Captions by John von Hartz. 181pp. 9¼ x 10¾. 23585-8 Pa. $12.95

INDIAN SIGN LANGUAGE, William Tomkins. Over 525 signs developed by Sioux and other tribes. Written instructions and diagrams. Also 290 pictographs. 111pp. 6⅛ x 9¼. 22029-X Pa. $3.95

ANATOMY: A Complete Guide for Artists, Joseph Sheppard. A master of figure drawing shows artists how to render human anatomy convincingly. Over 460 illustrations. 224pp. 8⅜ x 11¼. 27279-6 Pa. $10.95

MEDIEVAL CALLIGRAPHY: Its History and Technique, Marc Drogin. Spirited history, comprehensive instruction manual covers 13 styles (ca. 4th century thru 15th). Excellent photographs; directions for duplicating medieval techniques with modern tools. 224pp. 8⅜ x 11¼. 26142-5 Pa. $12.95

DRIED FLOWERS: How to Prepare Them, Sarah Whitlock and Martha Rankin. Complete instructions on how to use silica gel, meal and borax, perlite aggregate, sand and borax, glycerine and water to create attractive permanent flower arrangements. 12 illustrations. 32pp. 5⅜ x 8½. 21802-3 Pa. $1.00

EASY-TO-MAKE BIRD FEEDERS FOR WOODWORKERS, Scott D. Campbell. Detailed, simple-to-use guide for designing, constructing, caring for and using feeders. Text, illustrations for 12 classic and contemporary designs. 96pp. 5⅜ x 8½. 25847-5 Pa. $2.95

SCOTTISH WONDER TALES FROM MYTH AND LEGEND, Donald A. Mackenzie. 16 lively tales tell of giants rumbling down mountainsides, of a magic wand that turns stone pillars into warriors, of gods and goddesses, evil hags, powerful forces and more. 240pp. 5⅜ x 8½. 29677-6 Pa. $6.95

THE HISTORY OF UNDERCLOTHES, C. Willett Cunnington and Phyllis Cunnington. Fascinating, well-documented survey covering six centuries of English undergarments, enhanced with over 100 illustrations: 12th-century laced-up bodice, footed long drawers (1795), 19th-century bustles, l9th-century corsets for men, Victorian "bust improvers," much more. 272pp. 5⅜ x 8¼. 27124-2 Pa. $9.95

ARTS AND CRAFTS FURNITURE: The Complete Brooks Catalog of 1912, Brooks Manufacturing Co. Photos and detailed descriptions of more than 150 now very collectible furniture designs from the Arts and Crafts movement depict davenports, settees, buffets, desks, tables, chairs, bedsteads, dressers and more, all built of solid, quarter-sawed oak. Invaluable for students and enthusiasts of antiques, Americana and the decorative arts. 80pp. 6½ x 9¼. 27471-3 Pa. $8.95

HOW WE INVENTED THE AIRPLANE: An Illustrated History, Orville Wright. Fascinating firsthand account covers early experiments, construction of planes and motors, first flights, much more. Introduction and commentary by Fred C. Kelly. 76 photographs. 96pp. 8¼ x 11. 25662-6 Pa. $8.95

THE ARTS OF THE SAILOR: Knotting, Splicing and Ropework, Hervey Garrett Smith. Indispensable shipboard reference covers tools, basic knots and useful hitches; handsewing and canvas work, more. Over 100 illustrations. Delightful reading for sea lovers. 256pp. 5⅜ x 8½. 26440-8 Pa. $7.95

FRANK LLOYD WRIGHT'S FALLINGWATER: The House and Its History, Second, Revised Edition, Donald Hoffmann. A total revision—both in text and illustrations—of the standard document on Fallingwater, the boldest, most personal architectural statement of Wright's mature years, updated with valuable new material from the recently opened Frank Lloyd Wright Archives. "Fascinating"—*The New York Times*. 116 illustrations. 128pp. 9¼ x 10¾. 27430-6 Pa. $11.95

PHOTOGRAPHIC SKETCHBOOK OF THE CIVIL WAR, Alexander Gardner. 100 photos taken on field during the Civil War. Famous shots of Manassas Harper's Ferry, Lincoln, Richmond, slave pens, etc. 244pp. 10⅝ x 8¼. 22731-6 Pa. $9.95

FIVE ACRES AND INDEPENDENCE, Maurice G. Kains. Great back-to-the-land classic explains basics of self-sufficient farming. The one book to get. 95 illustrations. 397pp. 5⅜ x 8½.
20974-1 Pa. $7.95

SONGS OF EASTERN BIRDS, Dr. Donald J. Borror. Songs and calls of 60 species most common to eastern U.S.: warblers, woodpeckers, flycatchers, thrushes, larks, many more in high-quality recording. Cassette and manual 99912-2 $9.95

A MODERN HERBAL, Margaret Grieve. Much the fullest, most exact, most useful compilation of herbal material. Gigantic alphabetical encyclopedia, from aconite to zedoary, gives botanical information, medical properties, folklore, economic uses, much else. Indispensable to serious reader. 161 illustrations. 888pp. 6½ x 9¼. 2-vol. set. (USO)
Vol. I: 22798-7 Pa. $9.95
Vol. II: 22799-5 Pa. $9.95

HIDDEN TREASURE MAZE BOOK, Dave Phillips. Solve 34 challenging mazes accompanied by heroic tales of adventure. Evil dragons, people-eating plants, blood-thirsty giants, many more dangerous adversaries lurk at every twist and turn. 34 mazes, stories, solutions. 48pp. 8¼ x 11. 24566-7 Pa. $2.95

LETTERS OF W. A. MOZART, Wolfgang A. Mozart. Remarkable letters show bawdy wit, humor, imagination, musical insights, contemporary musical world; includes some letters from Leopold Mozart. 276pp. 5⅜ x 8½. 22859-2 Pa. $7.95

BASIC PRINCIPLES OF CLASSICAL BALLET, Agrippina Vaganova. Great Russian theoretician, teacher explains methods for teaching classical ballet. 118 illustrations. 175pp. 5⅜ x 8½.
22036-2 Pa. $5.95

THE JUMPING FROG, Mark Twain. Revenge edition. The original story of The Celebrated Jumping Frog of Calaveras County, a hapless French translation, and Twain's hilarious "retranslation" from the French. 12 illustrations. 66pp. 5⅜ x 8½.
22686-7 Pa. $3.95

BEST REMEMBERED POEMS, Martin Gardner (ed.). The 126 poems in this superb collection of 19th- and 20th-century British and American verse range from Shelley's "To a Skylark" to the impassioned "Renascence" of Edna St. Vincent Millay and to Edward Lear's whimsical "The Owl and the Pussycat." 224pp. 5⅜ x 8½.
27165-X Pa. $4.95

COMPLETE SONNETS, William Shakespeare. Over 150 exquisite poems deal with love, friendship, the tyranny of time, beauty's evanescence, death and other themes in language of remarkable power, precision and beauty. Glossary of archaic terms. 80pp. 5$\frac{3}{16}$ x 8¼.
26686-9 Pa. $1.00

BODIES IN A BOOKSHOP, R. T. Campbell. Challenging mystery of blackmail and murder with ingenious plot and superbly drawn characters. In the best tradition of British suspense fiction. 192pp. 5⅜ x 8½. 24720-1 Pa. $6.95

THE WIT AND HUMOR OF OSCAR WILDE, Alvin Redman (ed.). More than 1,000 ripostes, paradoxes, wisecracks: Work is the curse of the drinking classes; I can resist everything except temptation; etc. 258pp. 5⅜ x 8½.   20602-5 Pa. $5.95

SHAKESPEARE LEXICON AND QUOTATION DICTIONARY, Alexander Schmidt. Full definitions, locations, shades of meaning in every word in plays and poems. More than 50,000 exact quotations. 1,485pp. 6½ x 9¼. 2-vol. set.
Vol. 1: 22726-X Pa. $16.95
Vol. 2: 22727-8 Pa. $16.95

SELECTED POEMS, Emily Dickinson. Over 100 best-known, best-loved poems by one of America's foremost poets, reprinted from authoritative early editions. No comparable edition at this price. Index of first lines. 64pp. 5³⁄₁₆ x 8¼.
26466-1 Pa. $1.00

CELEBRATED CASES OF JUDGE DEE (DEE GOONG AN), translated by Robert van Gulik. Authentic 18th-century Chinese detective novel; Dee and associates solve three interlocked cases. Led to van Gulik's own stories with same characters. Extensive introduction. 9 illustrations. 237pp. 5⅜ x 8½.   23337-5 Pa. $6.95

THE MALLEUS MALEFICARUM OF KRAMER AND SPRENGER, translated by Montague Summers. Full text of most important witchhunter's "bible," used by both Catholics and Protestants. 278pp. 6⅝ x 10.   22802-9 Pa. $12.95

SPANISH STORIES/CUENTOS ESPAÑOLES: A Dual-Language Book, Angel Flores (ed.). Unique format offers 13 great stories in Spanish by Cervantes, Borges, others. Faithful English translations on facing pages. 352pp. 5⅜ x 8½.
25399-6 Pa. $8.95

THE CHICAGO WORLD'S FAIR OF 1893: A Photographic Record, Stanley Appelbaum (ed.). 128 rare photos show 200 buildings, Beaux-Arts architecture, Midway, original Ferris Wheel, Edison's kinetoscope, more. Architectural emphasis; full text. 116pp. 8¼ x 11.   23990-X Pa. $9.95

OLD QUEENS, N.Y., IN EARLY PHOTOGRAPHS, Vincent F. Seyfried and William Asadorian. Over 160 rare photographs of Maspeth, Jamaica, Jackson Heights, and other areas. Vintage views of DeWitt Clinton mansion, 1939 World's Fair and more. Captions. 192pp. 8⅞ x 11.   26358-4 Pa. $12.95

CAPTURED BY THE INDIANS: 15 Firsthand Accounts, 1750-1870, Frederick Drimmer. Astounding true historical accounts of grisly torture, bloody conflicts, relentless pursuits, miraculous escapes and more, by people who lived to tell the tale. 384pp. 5⅜ x 8½.   24901-8 Pa. $8.95

THE WORLD'S GREAT SPEECHES, Lewis Copeland and Lawrence W. Lamm (eds.). Vast collection of 278 speeches of Greeks to 1970. Powerful and effective models; unique look at history. 842pp. 5⅜ x 8½.   20468-5 Pa. $14.95

THE BOOK OF THE SWORD, Sir Richard F. Burton. Great Victorian scholar/adventurer's eloquent, erudite history of the "queen of weapons"–from prehistory to early Roman Empire. Evolution and development of early swords, variations (sabre, broadsword, cutlass, scimitar, etc.), much more. 336pp. 6⅛ x 9¼.
25434-8 Pa. $9.95

AUTOBIOGRAPHY: The Story of My Experiments with Truth, Mohandas K. Gandhi. Boyhood, legal studies, purification, the growth of the Satyagraha (nonviolent protest) movement. Critical, inspiring work of the man responsible for the freedom of India. 480pp. 5⅜ x 8½. (USO) 24593-4 Pa. $8.95

CELTIC MYTHS AND LEGENDS, T. W. Rolleston. Masterful retelling of Irish and Welsh stories and tales. Cuchulain, King Arthur, Deirdre, the Grail, many more. First paperback edition. 58 full-page illustrations. 512pp. 5⅜ x 8½. 26507-2 Pa. $9.95

THE PRINCIPLES OF PSYCHOLOGY, William James. Famous long course complete, unabridged. Stream of thought, time perception, memory, experimental methods; great work decades ahead of its time. 94 figures. 1,391pp. 5⅜ x 8½. 2-vol. set.
Vol. I: 20381-6 Pa. $12.95
Vol. II: 20382-4 Pa. $12.95

THE WORLD AS WILL AND REPRESENTATION, Arthur Schopenhauer. Definitive English translation of Schopenhauer's life work, correcting more than 1,000 errors, omissions in earlier translations. Translated by E. F. J. Payne. Total of 1,269pp. 5⅜ x 8½. 2-vol. set.
Vol. 1: 21761-2 Pa. $11.95
Vol. 2: 21762-0 Pa. $12.95

MAGIC AND MYSTERY IN TIBET, Madame Alexandra David-Neel. Experiences among lamas, magicians, sages, sorcerers, Bonpa wizards. A true psychic discovery. 32 illustrations. 321pp. 5⅜ x 8½. (USO) 22682-4 Pa. $8.95

THE EGYPTIAN BOOK OF THE DEAD, E. A. Wallis Budge. Complete reproduction of Ani's papyrus, finest ever found. Full hieroglyphic text, interlinear transliteration, word-for-word translation, smooth translation. 533pp. 6½ x 9¼.
21866-X Pa. $10.95

MATHEMATICS FOR THE NONMATHEMATICIAN, Morris Kline. Detailed, college-level treatment of mathematics in cultural and historical context, with numerous exercises. Recommended Reading Lists. Tables. Numerous figures. 641pp. 5⅜ x 8½.
24823-2 Pa. $11.95

THEORY OF WING SECTIONS: Including a Summary of Airfoil Data, Ira H. Abbott and A. E. von Doenhoff. Concise compilation of subsonic aerodynamic characteristics of NACA wing sections, plus description of theory. 350pp. of tables. 693pp. 5⅜ x 8½. 60586-8 Pa. $14.95

THE RIME OF THE ANCIENT MARINER, Gustave Doré, S. T. Coleridge. Doré's finest work; 34 plates capture moods, subtleties of poem. Flawless full-size reproductions printed on facing pages with authoritative text of poem. "Beautiful. Simply beautiful."–*Publisher's Weekly.* 77pp. 9¼ x 12. 22305-1 Pa. $6.95

NORTH AMERICAN INDIAN DESIGNS FOR ARTISTS AND CRAFTSPEOPLE, Eva Wilson. Over 360 authentic copyright-free designs adapted from Navajo blankets, Hopi pottery, Sioux buffalo hides, more. Geometrics, symbolic figures, plant and animal motifs, etc. 128pp. 8⅜ x 11. (EUK) 25341-4 Pa. $8.95

SCULPTURE: Principles and Practice, Louis Slobodkin. Step-by-step approach to clay, plaster, metals, stone; classical and modern. 253 drawings, photos. 255pp. 8⅛ x 11.
22960-2 Pa. $11.95

THE INFLUENCE OF SEA POWER UPON HISTORY, 1660–1783, A. T. Mahan. Influential classic of naval history and tactics still used as text in war colleges. First paperback edition. 4 maps. 24 battle plans. 640pp. 5⅜ x 8½.   25509-3 Pa. $12.95

THE STORY OF THE TITANIC AS TOLD BY ITS SURVIVORS, Jack Winocour (ed.). What it was really like. Panic, despair, shocking inefficiency, and a little heroism. More thrilling than any fictional account. 26 illustrations. 320pp. 5⅜ x 8½.
20610-6 Pa. $8.95

FAIRY AND FOLK TALES OF THE IRISH PEASANTRY, William Butler Yeats (ed.). Treasury of 64 tales from the twilight world of Celtic myth and legend: "The Soul Cages," "The Kildare Pooka," "King O'Toole and his Goose," many more. Introduction and Notes by W. B. Yeats. 352pp. 5⅜ x 8½.   26941-8 Pa. $8.95

BUDDHIST MAHAYANA TEXTS, E. B. Cowell and Others (eds.). Superb, accurate translations of basic documents in Mahayana Buddhism, highly important in history of religions. The Buddha-karita of Asvaghosha, Larger Sukhavativyuha, more. 448pp. 5⅜ x 8½.   25552-2 Pa. $12.95

ONE TWO THREE . . . INFINITY: Facts and Speculations of Science, George Gamow. Great physicist's fascinating, readable overview of contemporary science: number theory, relativity, fourth dimension, entropy, genes, atomic structure, much more. 128 illustrations. Index. 352pp. 5⅜ x 8½.   25664-2 Pa. $8.95

ENGINEERING IN HISTORY, Richard Shelton Kirby, et al. Broad, nontechnical survey of history's major technological advances: birth of Greek science, industrial revolution, electricity and applied science, 20th-century automation, much more. 181 illustrations. ". . . excellent . . ."–*Isis.* Bibliography. vii + 530pp. 5⅜ x 8¼.
26412-2 Pa. $14.95

DALÍ ON MODERN ART: The Cuckolds of Antiquated Modern Art, Salvador Dalí. Influential painter skewers modern art and its practitioners. Outrageous evaluations of Picasso, Cézanne, Turner, more. 15 renderings of paintings discussed. 44 calligraphic decorations by Dalí. 96pp. 5⅜ x 8½. (USO)   29220-7 Pa. $4.95

ANTIQUE PLAYING CARDS: A Pictorial History, Henry René D'Allemagne. Over 900 elaborate, decorative images from rare playing cards (14th–20th centuries): Bacchus, death, dancing dogs, hunting scenes, royal coats of arms, players cheating, much more. 96pp. 9¼ x 12¼.   29265-7 Pa. $11.95

MAKING FURNITURE MASTERPIECES: 30 Projects with Measured Drawings, Franklin H. Gottshall. Step-by-step instructions, illustrations for constructing handsome, useful pieces, among them a Sheraton desk, Chippendale chair, Spanish desk, Queen Anne table and a William and Mary dressing mirror. 224pp. 8⅛ x 11¼.
29338-6 Pa. $13.95

THE FOSSIL BOOK: A Record of Prehistoric Life, Patricia V. Rich et al. Profusely illustrated definitive guide covers everything from single-celled organisms and dinosaurs to birds and mammals and the interplay between climate and man. Over 1,500 illustrations. 760pp. 7½ x 10⅛.   29371-8 Pa. $29.95

Prices subject to change without notice.

Available at your book dealer or write for free catalog to Dept. GI, Dover Publications, Inc., 31 East 2nd St., Mineola, N.Y. 11501. Dover publishes more than 500 books each year on science, elementary and advanced mathematics, biology, music, art, literary history, social sciences and other areas.